T0244619

Thriving as an Online K-12 Educator

Thriving as an Online K-12 Educator is the perfect all-in-one guide to taking your K-12 class online. We know, now more than ever, that teachers have not been equally or systematically trained and resourced to make a sudden transition to online or blended instruction. This concise, accessible book collects time-tested strategies and fresh perspectives from experienced educators to help you smooth out even the most abrupt shift to technology-enhanced teaching and learning. With these insights into institutional supports, effective digital tools, equitable practice, social-emotional considerations, and beyond, you will be better prepared than ever to help your students thrive in online and blended learning environments.

Jody Peerless Green is a teacher on special assignment (TOSA) as an academic coach focusing on educational technology at La Habra City School District, Orange County, CA, USA.

Other Eye On Education Books
Available From Routledge (www.routledge.com/k-12)

Making Technology Work in Schools:
How PK-12 Educators Can Foster Digital-Age Learning
Timothy D. Green, Loretta C. Donovan, and Jody Peerless Green

Integrating Computer Science Across the Core:
Strategies for K-12 Districts
Tom Liam Lynch, Gerald Ardito, and Pam Amendola

The Genius Hour Guidebook:
Fostering Passion, Wonder, and Inquiry in
the Classroom, 2nd edition
Denise Krebs and Gallit Zvi

Tech Request:
A Guide for Coaching Educators in the Digital World
Emily L. Davis and Brad Currie

Universal Design for Learning in the Early Childhood Classroom:
Teaching Children of all Languages, Cultures, and Abilities,
Birth–8 Years
Pamela Brillante and Karen Nemeth

Coding as a Playground:
Programming and Computational Thinking
in the Early Childhood Classroom, 2nd edition
Marina Umaschi Bers

Thriving as an Online K-12 Educator

Essential Practices
from the Field

Edited by Jody Peerless Green

Routledge
Taylor & Francis Group

NEW YORK AND LONDON

First published 2021
by Routledge
52 Vanderbilt Avenue, New York, NY 10017

and by Routledge
2 Park Square, Milton Park, Abingdon, Oxon, OX14 4RN

*Routledge is an imprint of the Taylor & Francis Group,
an informa business*

Library of Congress Cataloging-in-Publication Data
A catalog record for this book has been requested

ISBN: 978-0-367-65057-5 (hbk)
ISBN: 978-0-367-64094-1 (pbk)
ISBN: 978-1-003-12763-5 (ebk)

Typeset in Palatino
by Apex CoVantage, LLC

Contents

Introduction

When schools shut down in March of 2020, students, teachers, and families in urban and rural schools, districts large and small, were put in a situation that most would never have thought possible. School and district leadership were under pressure to solve multiple problems in a record amount of time, including: How do we provide a continuation of learning? Do we send packets home or do we try to go digital? If we provide instruction digitally, how do we ensure all students have devices and continuous tech support? How do we prepare our teachers to teach entirely online? How many hours of instruction per day should we plan for? In what ways do we deliver that instruction? There were, and there continue to be, more questions than answers.

As leadership prepared the technology and the overall plan for what distance learning should look like, teachers across the country (across the world, really) launched into crisis teaching mode. While most teachers felt ill-prepared for the task of teaching remotely, regardless of how much district support and training was provided, they nonetheless rose to the challenge of communicating, teaching, connecting, and assessing students via distance learning, remote teaching, or whatever name it took on. Teachers' main concern, even more than "I don't know how to do this!", was (and continues to be) centered around students who face barriers to participating in distance learning. We all have students who come to school to be fed and to feel safe. We all have students who would rather be at school than at home for a variety of reasons. We all have students who do not have the supplies, devices, or support they need in order to be successful in distance learning. And most glaringly, we all have students for whom the inequity in education placed a hard stop on their ability to participate. This book can't solve all of these issues, but it can help to provide some guidance for teachers within the elements we are able to control, such as how we work to engage our students in equitable ways.

The impetus for writing a book to help teachers adjust to life as a "short-notice online teacher" was a global pandemic, but we hope that these ideas will take you beyond that. Our goal is that this book will help to move teachers from crisis mode into "this is just how it's done now" mode. When this project started, it looked like education would remain entirely online for the fall. Some universities had already made that decision, and it seemed as if K-12 would follow suit. However, most districts are now looking to provide a hybrid program for their students (in some cases, that includes an online academy), and we shifted our focus to be more of a blended approach to instruction in order that we don't find ourselves caught off-guard if we have to shut down with little notice in the future. We provide background, knowledge, and plans for helping teachers understand the resources available, how to access those resources, and how to engage students and families in the work of a hybrid approach to learning. Within these pages, we hope to push your thinking with ideas you might not have known about or considered before by providing a wide variety of topics and resources for continued learning and connection.

This book is a collection of educational technology experiences and approaches. It contains big, passionate ideas about the opportunities we now have in education to provide better instruction for students in both brick-and-mortar and online environments, as well as deliberate strategies for achieving these ambitions. The book begins with a mindset framework to help educators consider how to provide distance education opportunities for students in face-to-face and digital classrooms. It then shifts to a discussion about how to best engage students in the learning with various strategies and resources, and then moves to the more interpersonal parts of distance and hybrid learning. It ends with advice for making deeper connections for families and for yourself as a professional.

Each chapter is written by expert authors who will share their experiences and passions with you as they weave their own stories within their respective chapters. Our authors are educators from coast to coast and everywhere in between. Despite our geographical differences and the wide variety of backgrounds and job descriptions, our experiences with emergency online teaching due to the COVID-19 pandemic have been remarkably similar. What binds us together most is that we all share a love for teaching and learning, technology integration, teachers, and most of all, students.

Contributors

Gloria Cazarez is currently a 1st/2nd grade teacher in a multi-age classroom in California. She has been working in education for over ten years and is working on attaining her master's degree in multilingual and multicultural education. In her spare time, she serves on local boards and works with nonprofits that serve the migrant multilingual community.

Nyree Clark is a curriculum program specialist in technology PreK-6 for the Colton Joint Unified School District. Her journey in education began in 1998 and has been referred to as her "dream job" thereafter. She has been a reading recovery teacher, gifted and talented education certified teacher, reading specialist teacher on assignment, and has earned multiple certificates and ambassadorships in the field of educational technology. She has taught kindergarten to 4th grade and currently works at the district level to support teachers, students, and staff in the integration and implementation of technology to increase student achievement and productivity. She is a member of the African American Parent Advisory Committee (bit.ly/AAPAC_CJUSD), which focuses on amplifying the voices of the African American students and parents in the school district. Professionally, Nyree was awarded the Technology Innovator of the Year 2020 through Inland Area CUE affiliate and is a TOSAChat moderator supporting teachers on special assignment worldwide. She is a co-founding member of Equity in Action CA (bit.ly/EquityInActionCA), a group of educators researching and implementing ways to diversify technology conferences and professional learning settings. She excels in making connections with people across the globe and states, "I love this new technology-rich world and the tools in which we are able to amplify the voices of the unheard."

Stephanie Filardo (@i3lagebra) is a math teacher, professional development provider, ISTE Certified Educator, METC Planning and Advisory Committee Member, Google Certified Innovator (#COL16) and Trainer, ISTE Ignite presenter (2017, 2018), trauma survivor, and flawed human being. She has previously taught computer science (high school) and special education (elementary/ high school levels). Stephanie uses technology to differentiate and take new approaches to the curriculum. She enjoys helping teachers solve problems and rethink their classrooms using technology.

Anthony Gabriele is currently the Assistant to the Superintendent for Learning and Innovation in the Centennial School District, located outside of Philadelphia, PA, as well as senior adjunct faculty and the technology coordinator for the University of Pennsylvania's Penn Literacy Network. Throughout his career, Anthony has worked as the Supervisor of Learning, Development, and Professional Growth for the Garnet Valley School District, a 7-12 English language arts teacher, and a K-12 instructional staff developer for the Wissahickon School District, with a specific focus on integrating literacy, technology, and curriculum. Anthony also worked with the Pennsylvania Department of Education to build PA Core aligned instructional frameworks and assessments and, in partnership with Apple, iTunes University Open Education courses to support educators in their work with the PA Core standards. Currently, Anthony is the district lead on working with the US Department of Education on the #GoOpen movement. For more information, you can visit www. anthonyjgabriele.com.

Dr. Edward Gonzalez is a K-12 teacher, university lecturer, and keynote speaker. As the proud recipient of the Computer Using Educators 2018 LeRoy Finkle Fellow and the California State University, Fullerton 2016 Edwin Carr Fellow, he strives to give underserved K-12 students the opportunity to lead in the classroom and at the university level. In his circles, he is recognized for facilitating children-led professional development for adults. You can find Edward regularly presenting at the National CUE Conference and the International Society for Technology in Education.

Dr. Tim Green is a former K-12 teacher who has been a professor of educational technology and a teacher educator at California State University, Fullerton since 1999. Five of these years he served as the Director of Distance Education at CSUF. He has co-directed and taught in an online MS in educational technology program since 2010 (www.fullerton.edu/edtech). He is the author of numerous articles and books, as well as a presenter about online distance education, instructional design, and the integration of educational technology. His latest books include *Making Technology Work in Schools: How PK-12 Educators Can Foster Digital-Age Learning* (Green, Donovan, & Green, Routledge) and *The Essentials of Instructional Design: Connecting Fundamental Principles With Process and Practice, 4th Edition* (Brown & Green, Routledge), which earned the Outstanding Book Award (2016) for the Design and Development Division of the Association for Educational Communications and Technology (AECT). He has co-produced a podcast since 2013 on trends and issues in instructional design, educational technology, and learning sciences. The podcast (trendsandissues.com) won the Association for Educational Communications and Technology Immersive Learning Award (2014). In 2019 he won the ISTE Teacher Education Network Award for Excellence in Teacher Education. Dr. Green earned his PhD in instructional systems technology with a minor in curriculum and instruction from Indiana University. You can connect with Dr. Green on Twitter @theEdTechDoctor.

Josh Harris is an educator who is passionate about bringing equity to all students through the use of and access to digital tools and the global community of learners. He has been in public education since 1999, starting as an ASL interpreter. From 2000 to 2013 he wore many different classroom hats, and taught nearly everything you can teach in a middle school. In 2013 he left the classroom to become an education technology specialist (TOSA), supporting over 150 teachers in K-12. In 2016, he joined the Alisal Union School District, an elementary district in Salinas, CA, to become the Director of Educational Technology. In 2020 he was recognized as the CUE Administrator of the Year for the work of his team of TOSAs. In addition to being an authorized Google for Education Certified Trainer and Innovator, he is a lover of all canines and is an avocational art historian. Josh loves working with teachers and schools from all over: feel free to reach out on Twitter (@edtech-spec) or email (josh@edtechspec.org) for any reason whatsoever, even just to say "hi."

Lynn Kleinmeyer is a digital learning consultant for Grant Wood Area Education Agency, an educational service agency serving school districts in eastern Iowa. In her work as a digital learning consultant, Lynn works with districts to embrace the potential of digital learning, as well as working with districts exploring openly licensed educational resources (OER) and providing professional learning and support for teacher librarians. Prior to her consultancy work, Lynn taught 7th grade reading for 14 years before becoming a teacher librarian. You can find Lynn on Twitter: @THLibrariZen.

Susan Stewart K-2 Can, TOO is the motto of this lead learner! Susan Stewart has been in education for 21 years. She is currently the K-12 Instructional Technology Coach for Fowler Unified School District in Central California. Within her district, Susan has facilitated the implementation of a 1:1 program using iPads, Chromebooks, and the Google Suite. She regularly works with individual and teams of teachers to promote best practices for using technology to enhance instruction, foster creativity, support and supplement content, and improve assessment. In addition to her responsibilities with Fowler Unified, Susan regularly speaks on blended learning and classroom technology at professional learning events and in school districts throughout North America. Susan is a Keynote Speaker, a Google Education Innovator and Trainer, and a Seesaw Ambassador. She serves on the board for CVCUE, a California non-profit organization that promotes innovation in education. Follow Susan on Twitter @TechCoachSusan.

Knikole Taylor is a professional development trainer, curriculum developer, author, and speaker who has been privileged to travel the world to speak and work with other educators at conferences, campuses, and district-wide events. It is her firm belief that anyone can succeed with tailored support. Knikole works to assist educators in being their best for the students and teachers they serve each day. Knikole also holds many industry designations including

Google Certified Trainer, Google Innovator, and Microsoft Innovative Educator Trainer, and she serves as co-leader of GEG North Texas. She received her bachelor's from Texas A&M-Commerce and her masters of education in administration from Lamar University. Knikole is currently a doctoral student at Dallas Baptist University pursuing her EdD in educational leadership.

Yaritza Villalba is President and Founder of YV Educational Resources Inc., a nonprofit 501(c)3 dedicated to assisting educators and students from around the world, and has ten years of experience in education. She started her career teaching social studies to high school students in Bedford-Stuyvesant, Brooklyn, NY. Throughout the years she has executed and developed culturally responsive curricula and conducted a variety of professional development for educators throughout the United States. She is currently a peer collaborative teacher at an alternative high school in Bedford-Stuyvesant, teaching over-aged and under-credited students history and civics through a critical lens. Her overall mission in education is to provide teachers and students with an array of strategies and materials to assist them in the educational process and connect to the world around them. You can find and collaborate with Yaritza through Twitter @inc_yv or if you would prefer a more intimate collaborative opportunity, you can check out her nonprofit's website at www.yveducationalresources.com and become a member, with full access to free materials and PBL tasks for your diverse classroom of student learners.

Hue-An Wren, EdD, is a teacher on special assignment in the K-12 Office of Instructional Technology at Garden Grove Unified School District. Prior to that she was an elementary teacher for 12 years where she was able to implement technology with students as young as kindergarten. During her time in the classroom, she worked as an instructional coach to advise teachers on best practices in curriculum and pedagogy. She is also a Google Certified Innovator and enjoys working in this community to bring best practices in digital learning to the district. Hue-An earned her doctorate in learning technologies from Pepperdine University. Her research focuses on using digital online communities to teach writing skills.

1

Distance Education in K-12

Guiding Practice Through a Shared Definition and Framework

Tim Green

My first experience with distance education took place unwittingly in the fall of 1994 when I was a high school substitute teacher for two months for a teacher who taught information technology. The teacher was responsible for five classes of information technology at different levels—basic and advanced—for students in grades 7–12. The classes focused on word processing, spreadsheets, databases, and desktop publishing. They were taught in a rather sophisticated, at that time, computer lab equipped with 35 desktop PCs and a teacher desktop PC connected to an LCD panel that sat on top of an overhead projector to project what was on the teacher's computer screen. This was amazing technology, when it didn't overheat and stop working. Another amazing technology connected to the teacher's computer, which I accidently discovered was a modem connected to a phone line. I was thrilled when I discovered this because I could check my AOL email at lunch time! The one email I received daily. What does this all have to do with distance education? Hang with me—I am getting to it.

After a month of following the daily routine of the course that consisted of students using software to replicate a series of steps from a handout and then printing out the results to turn in, I decided to mix things up and add in another technology-based activity. I decided to introduce the students to online bulletin board systems (BBS) and use one to conduct an inquiry activity. The outcome was to determine where a friend of mine lived and what he did for an occupation (in case you wanted to know, he was a computer science graduate student at a university about 30 miles away). We used the modem to log on to the internet and connect to a BBS to leave him yes/no questions and to read the responses he left us. Unwittingly, for three weeks, I involved my students in a distance education experience. I won't go into how I got into hot water for the long-distance costs incurred in doing this.

My second experience with distance education was in 1996 as a graduate student at Indiana University. I was fortunate to be an associate instructor who had the opportunity to teach five educators enrolled in a semester-long course on instructional media production that required them to design and develop a handout, a HyperCard stack, and a single webpage (go ahead, look up HyperCard). The course was facilitated using a mixture of analog and digital technologies: email, the telephone, postal mail, and a fax machine. Content was provided through a textbook along with a syllabus mailed to students before the start of the semester. Students worked independently. There was no set weekly schedule that required students to check in with each other or with me—there were only project due dates. My primary role was to answer questions and provide feedback on the projects when students contacted me, which I did primarily through email and the occasional phone call.

I contrast these experiences with my current experience teaching at a distance. I co-direct and teach in a graduate-level educational technology program for educators that runs completely online using a learning management system (LMS) and a mixture of analog and digital technologies to deliver content and engage learners. The learners take ten semester-long courses over 16 months to earn their degree. Each course runs for 16 weeks with a set weekly schedule. The learners are highly engaged asynchronously and synchronously with each other and with their instructors. My role when I teach a course is a facilitator who guides my learners through the experience by sharing my expertise, by providing formative and summative feedback, and by modifying the learning experience whenever necessary.

I share these experiences to highlight three points. The first is that as of the writing of this chapter, I have been involved in distance education for 26 years. During these years, I have been a distance education learner, instructor, researcher, and administrator. I have seen and been part of many changes that have occurred in distance education. This leads me to my second point. Despite these changes, the fundamental concept of distance education has remained the same. The critical attributes that define distance education have remained stable. Although distance education as a concept has not fundamentally changed, what has changed are the forms that it has taken. This leads me to my third point. Distance education throughout the years has been applied in different forms as analog and digital technologies have changed and as our understanding of teaching and learning has advanced.

Two Foundational Constructs: A Definition and a Framework

My experience as a distance education practitioner and researcher has led me to understand that there are two foundational constructs that are important for educators to consider and understand if we are to design and deliver effective distance education for our learners. These constructs are related to points two and three that I made in the previous paragraph. The two constructs focus on understanding what distance education is (the definition) and what elements are involved with creating distance education experiences that are equitable and inclusive (a framework).

I describe my perspectives of these two constructs in the remaining sections. My primary intent is to provide a foundation that can serve as a starting point for understanding and exploring distance education. Discussing a definition allows us to arrive at a shared understanding that makes it possible to have important conversations that can lead to improving our practice. Offering a framework provides us with a structure for exploring critical elements that must be attended to when we design and implement distance education experiences.

As you read the remaining parts of the chapter, keep in mind that it is not my intent to persuade or convince you to my way of thinking. I am aware that some reading this chapter may not agree with how I view distance education. I am fine with this because I believe that healthy disagreement can lead to productive dialogue. What I do hope is that you will consider the definition you have for distance education and how this definition influences how you view and engage in teaching at a distance and the distance education experiences your students participate in.

Toward a Shared Understanding: Defining Distance Education

The field of education is inundated with acronyms and terms. Although we use many of these with regularity, this does not guarantee that we have a shared understanding of what they actually mean. This is highly problematic because the understanding we have influences how these acronyms and terms are used—namely, how the terms are applied in practice.

There are a number of examples to draw from that illustrate this point. Personalized learning is one that immediately comes to my mind; it is currently a highly popular term that most educators have experienced. The term dates back to the 1960s and has made a resurgence during the past two decades. Personalized learning is focused on providing customized learning experiences that address "the distinct learning needs, interests, aspirations, or cultural backgrounds of individual students" with the goal of facilitating student academic success (Great Schools Partnership, 2015, para. 1). To achieve this goal, a wide variety of applications have been developed and implemented with the intent of personalizing learning. These applications have ranged from reconfiguring large schools into a school-within-a-school to developing learning pathways to implementing instructional methods like project-based learning to integrating technology to providing students with a voice in what occurs in the classroom. Because of the varying applications, it has become "difficult to determine precisely what the term is referring to when it is used without qualification, specific examples, or additional explanation" (Great Schools Partnership, 2015, para. 4). This has led to debates that tend to focus on the applications of personalized learning rather than on the general concept of personalized learning (Great Schools Partnership, 2015). A result is a lack of shared understanding of what personalized learning is, and, I would argue, has also resulted in ineffective applications of "personalized learning."

I shared the example of personalized learning because I believe that distance education has followed a comparable path. Throughout its long history, a wide variety of applications of distance education have been developed and implemented. Because of these varying applications, discussion and debate about distance education has often centered on the applications rather than on the specific concept of distance education and its critical attributes. Similar to personalized learning, this has led to a lack of clarity and a shared understanding about what distance education is. Further, this has led to ineffective applications of distance education, and in some cases it has led to applications that should not be considered distance education.

It is important that educators examine the definition of distance education because it will help bring clarity to the concept and bring us to a shared understanding. Subsequently, this will assist us in identifying the elements that are necessary to consider when designing and delivering distance education experiences. I believe that if educators understand the critical attributes that define distance education, we will better recognize and make sense of other terms that are often used synonymously to describe distance education, but should not be. A shared understanding will lead to meaningful dialogue that will improve our distance education practice and ultimately the educational experiences of our learners, which should be the critical outcome we are striving toward.

Two Cautions

I provide two cautions before we examine the definition and its critical attributes. Over the years, the definition of distance education has evolved (and no doubt will continue to evolve). This is not surprising when you realize it has a history that dates back to the late 19th century. The definitions of distance education have developed based on different perspectives that have been influenced by changes in education, events and shifts occurring in society, the advancement of technology, and the introduction of new theory and research findings. Despite the evolution of the definition, the critical attributes have remained relatively stable. It is important to be aware, though, that although these definitions are similar and share critical attributes, I do not believe that they are all equal. Often, a definition has one or two missing critical attributes.

The second caution is that a number of terms have been used to describe distance education. We need to be cautious about these terms and examine the attributes that define the terms. What we find when we do is that the terms are actually applications of distance education rather than definitions of what distance education is. A number of these terms come to mind—blended learning, e-learning, flipped learning, hybrid learning, online education, online learning, remote learning, virtual education, and virtual schooling. These are derivatives of the concept of distance education—again, they are applications of distance education. Even those these terms are often used synonymously to refer to distance education, they should not be. With these two cautions in mind, let's discuss the definition.

The Definition

There are four critical attributes that make up the definition I subscribe to when I refer to the concept of distance education. Before you read the definition and we parse out the attributes, I admit that the definition does not roll off the tongue easily. In spite of this, I prefer this definition because I believe it delineates the most essential elements that that educators must consider when designing and implementing effective distance education.

> Distance education is "institution-based, formal education where the learning group is separated, and where interactive telecommunication systems are used to connect learners, resources, and instructors."
>
> (Schlosser & Simonson, 2010, p. 1)

Let's break down each critical attribute of the definition.

◆ *Institution-based, formal education.* This attribute is often missing in definitions of distance education. I find his attribute causes the most contentious discussions. The focus of this attribute, as it is described, is that distance education is formal education (e.g., a degree program, a course, a planned lesson) that is provided by or in an accredited educational organization (e.g., a university, a County Office of Education, a K-12 school). The attribute differentiates formal learning experiences with experiences that an individual engages in for self-study or informal learning. This is important because it indicates that distance education fits within a system that has considered the educational purpose and the necessary support structures (e.g., community outreach, funding, professional development, technology support) needed to realize this purpose. Although this attribute may seem unnecessary or contentious, I believe it is important to include because it implies the need for thoughtful consideration of the purpose and the intentional and systematic planning of distance education. Contrast this notion with what took place worldwide in education during early 2020—it is rather easy to observe that much of what took place was not true distance education. It was, in most cases, emergency remote teaching (Hodges, Moore, Lockee, Trust, & Bond, 2020) delivered using "panic-gogy" (Kamenetz, 2020).

- *Learner group is separated.* This attribute indicates that the learners and the instructor are separated. Generally, separation is thought of in terms of location where the instructor is in one location while learners are in a different location or different locations. Separation can also be thought of in terms of time when the learners access the experience, with learners generally engaging asynchronously at times that are convenient to them. Simonson, Zvacek, and Smaldino (2019) write that the "separation of the student and the teacher is a fundamental characteristic of distance education" (p. 27). I believe this is the most common attribute that comes to mind when an educator comes across the term *distance education.*

- *Interactive telecommunications systems.* Telecommunications by definition is "communicating over a distance" (Merriam-Webster, n.d.). Considering this definition, this attribute implies that distance education includes the availability and use of analog and digital communication tools that allow learners to communicate in different forms with the instructor and with other learners in their group. I add that, due to the availability of communication tools and the internet, opportunities also exist for learners to communicate with others beyond the instructor and those in their learner group. The key element of this attribution is that communication is possible.

- *Connect learners, resources, and instructors.* The implication of this attribute is that there is a need for a clear instructional plan that is created using instructional design principles. The focus of the plan is on the instruction that promotes student learning. This includes the engagement of the instructor and learners and the learners with each other, the instructional resources learners have available, instructions that guide learners through specific learning activities, and how learners will be assessed and evaluated. These are all elements that we consider as educators when we design face-to-face instruction; they need to be carefully considered in distance education because learners often need increased scaffolding in a distance education environment because of the separation that exists.

Distance Education: An Umbrella Term

I consider distance education to be an umbrella term that encompasses a number of terms that are applications of distance education. These applications are on a continuum of experiences that can range from distance education programs like a virtual high school run completely online with limited to no face-to-face interactions to a one-time distance education experience like a Mystery Skype that takes place online and synchronously in a traditional face-to-face classroom. Although these experiences vary in their complexity, both are applications of distance education. No matter the complexity of the experience, for it to be considered distance education it must include the four critical attributes described in the previous section. As Simonson, Smaldino, Albright, and Zvacek (2009) indicated, "If one or more are missing, then the event is something different, if only slightly, than distance education" (p. 33).

The Design of Distance Education Experiences: Exploring a Framework

As I mentioned in the previous section, having a clear understanding of the critical attributes that define distance education brings clarity to the concept and assists us in identifying the elements that are necessary for effective distance education experiences. This may sound rational, but what does this look like in practice? The approach I take is based on a framework (see Figure 1.1) that I developed that offers a structure for considering the critical elements that must be attended to when we design and implement distance education experiences. The framework is based on a combination of several elements: my experience creating and facilitating distance education experiences, my work supporting others as they have done the same, research I have conducted, and research I have read.

The Distance Educator Mindset Ecosystem

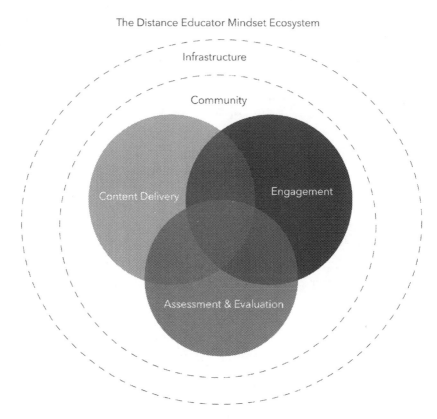

FIGURE 1.1 The Distance Education Mindset Ecosystem Framework. A graphical representation of the elements that define the framework.

Source: Framework and image created by Tim Green, PhD © 2015

The framework includes five elements: infrastructure, community, content delivery, engagement, and assessment and evaluation. The complex relationship of three primary elements—content delivery, engagement, and assessment and evaluation—is at the heart of the framework. These elements are multifaceted. Educators who are acutely skilled at teaching at a distance are able to successfully attend to these three elements at the same time. These educators have a *distance educator mindset* (Green, 2015) that includes values, beliefs, dispositions, knowledge, and skills that permit them to design and deliver equitable and inclusive experiences for their learners. An educator who has a distance educator mindset is capable of providing power-ful learning anytime, anywhere through technology (Green & Donovan, 2018).

The Framework Elements

Let's take a look at the five elements that make up the frame-work. My goal is to describe the framework elements in a general sense and point out how they fit together. I also share a few questions to consider about each element. It is beyond the scope of this chapter to discuss the elements in depth, which would include making connections to the research (I'll have to leave this for another project). There are two important aspects I would like you to consider as you explore the framework. One: the three overlapping center elements are grounded in Universal Design for Learning (UDL) principles (CAST, 2018). Two: the framework can be used by a single educator in a classroom or by a group of educators who are part of larger system such as a school district.

Infrastructure

Infrastructure refers primarily to two components: technology and support. Technology includes the analog and digital tools that are available to deliver distance education. Support includes the structures in place that provide technical, pedagogical, and administrative support along with students services. The level of support and services needed would depend, of course, on the application of distance education—that is, more and varied support would be needed to run an online virtual elementary school than would be needed to conduct a synchronous virtual field trip in a classroom.

A few questions I suggest asking when thinking about the infrastructure are:

- What technology do I have available?
- Who is in charge of making decisions about technology?
- How comfortable am I using the technology?
- What access do my learners have to technology—at school and at home?

- How comfortable are my learners with using the technology?
- What technical support is available for my learners?
- What support—technical and pedagogical—is available to me?
- What other support might my learners or I need?

Community

Community refers to the connectedness learners feel to each other and their instructor. It also includes how connected learners feel to their school. A strong sense of community generally occurs when learners feel valued and feel that their needs are being met. Community building will be addressed in different ways depending on whether we are considering distance education in a classroom or in a larger system such as an entire school or district. Building community refers to those activities and components that help learners feel connected. In the framework, community is embedded within infrastructure because the infrastructure available often has an impact on how community is built and maintained.

A few questions I suggest asking when thinking about community are:

- What are the values and beliefs I have about community?
- What are the values and beliefs my learners have about community?
- What does a strong community of learners look like to me?
- How will I help my learners feel valued?
- How will I make sure that my learners feel safe?
- How will I help my learners stay connected to me?
- How will I help my learners stay connected to each other?

Content Delivery

This element focuses on providing information and content to learners. I make a distinction between information and content. Information includes instructions, directions, and other types of information learners need to participate and to engage in distance education. Content focuses on the subject matter and other resources related to helping learners meet learning outcomes. It is important when considering content delivery to follow the UDL principle of multiple means of representation— providing learners with various avenues of access to information and content. Often, this means providing information and content in media formats (e.g., audio, images) other than text.

A few questions I suggest asking when thinking about content delivery are:

- ◆ What information do learners need to know and access in order to engage in a learning activity?
- ◆ What is the content that learners need to access?
- ◆ How will learners access this information and content?
- ◆ How do I provide information and content using multiple means of representation?
- ◆ Will I need to develop my own media?
- ◆ Are there open educational resources that I can use?

Engagement

Engagement focuses on how learners are involved in the various aspects of a distance education experience. When considering learner engagement, it is important to consider the UDL principle of providing multiple means of engagement. Implementing this principle can lead to learners who are actively involved and vested in their learning. Learners who are actively engaged will sustain their involvement over time. I believe it is important to differentiate between engagement and participation. Participation does not necessarily mean that a learner is engaged. I believe that a learner who participates may complete an activity but may not necessarily be invested in their learning. Engagement implies a deeper level of involvement.

A few questions I suggest asking when thinking about engagement are:

- ◆ What does learner engagement look like to me?
- ◆ What types of engagement will I have my learners involved in?

- ◆ What type of learning activities will I create to engage my learners in the content?
- ◆ What type of learning activities will I create to engage my learners with each other?
- ◆ What type of learning activities will I create to engage my learners with me?
- ◆ Will they engage with others outside of the class?

Assessment and Evaluation

This element focuses on learning outcomes and determining the level at which learners are meeting these outcomes. I purposefully have included assessment and evaluation to indicate that learners need to be provided with formative and summative feedback if they are to truly improve their learning. With this in mind, it is important to consider the UDL principle of providing for multiple means of action and expression. Learners need to be given multiple and varied opportunities to demonstrate their understanding and skills

A few questions I suggesting asking when thinking about assessment and evaluation are:

- ◆ What are the major learning outcomes?
- ◆ Is it clear what is expected of learners?
- ◆ Do learning outcomes require learners to demonstrate understanding at different depths of knowledge?
- ◆ Have I provided learners with options on how to demonstrate what they know and are able to do?
- ◆ Have I provided students with different types of feedback?
- ◆ How have I provided students with formative feedback to guide their learning and performance?
- ◆ Are learners given opportunities to practice and revise?

When looking at the framework, it is important to notice that content delivery, engagement, and assessment and evaluation are embedded within the infrastructure and community elements. This indicates that they are directly impacted by these two elements. Notice, as well, the overlap of content delivery, engagement, and assessment and evaluation. This shows that these multifaceted elements are interconnected. Where all three elements overlap is ideally where we should aim to be. This overlap implies that content delivery, engagement, and assessment and evaluation have been collectively considered, which will result in an effective distance education experience.

Moving Forward

The sudden move away from teaching face-to-face during early 2020 shined a direct spotlight on the need for educators to have a clear understanding of what it means for us to teach effectively at a distance. This statement is not an insinuation that we were all unprepared to move to teaching at a distance or that all teaching that took place was ineffective. Rather, this is an acknowledgement that we were, for the most part, caught off-guard with little time to adequately plan and prepare. As we reflect on what took place and look toward the future, we must make opportunities to engage in conversations, share, ask questions, examine research-based best practices, and learn from our collective experiences.

I believe we need to seize the opportunity presented by the circumstances thrust on us to better prepare ourselves to provide distance education experiences that are equitable and inclusive. We need to have a shared understanding of what distance education is and be able to describe the elements we need to plan for when designing and implementing distance education experiences. We cannot simply take what has been done in traditional face-to-face classrooms and superimpose it on a distance education environment. As Swan (2003) noted when discussing the research on distance education, "Trying to make online education 'the same' most likely will lead to less than optimal learning, when, in fact, online education has the potential to support significant paradigm changes in teaching and learning" (p. 3). We should welcome this potential and the challenges it brings because, as Swan wrote, we have the potential to transform teaching and learning. This will, however, require that we educators change our mindset and approach. Those who embrace this challenge will develop a *distance educator mindset* that is capable of providing powerful learning anytime, anywhere through technology (Green & Donovan, 2018).

References

CAST. (2018). *Universal design for learning guidelines version 2.2.* Cast. Retrieved from http://udlguidelines.cast.org

Great Schools Partnership. (2015, May 15). *Personalized learning.* The Glossary of Education Reform. Retrieved from www.edglossary. org/personalized-learning/

Green, T. (2015). *The distance educator mindset: A definition.* The Distance Educator Mindset. Retrieved from www. thedistanceeducatormindset.com/

Green, T., & Donovan, L. (2018). Rethinking teaching and learning for the iMaker Generation. In G. Hall, L. F. Quinn, & D. M. Gollnick (Eds.), *The handbook on teaching and learning.* Hoboken, NJ: Wiley Press.

Hodges, C., Moore, S., Lockee, B., Trust, T., & Bond, A. (2020). The difference between emergency remote teaching and online learning. *Educause Review, 27.*

Kamenetz, A. (2020, March 19). *"Panic-gogy": Teaching online classes during the coronavirus pandemic.* NPR. Retrieved from www.npr. org/2020/03/19/817885991/panic-gogy-teaching-online-classes-during-the-coronavirus-pandemic

Merriam-Webster. (n.d.). Telecommunication. In *Merriam-Webster.com dictionary.* Retrieved June 30, 2020, from www.merriam-webster. com/dictionary/telecommunication

Schlosser, L. A., & Simonson, M. (2010). *Distance education: Definition and glossary of terms* (3rd. ed.). Charlotte, NC: Information Age Publishing.

Simonson, M., Smaldino, S., Albright, M., & Zvacek, S. (2009). *Teaching and learning at a distance: Foundations of distance education.* Charlotte, NC: Information Age Publishing.

Simonson, M., Zvacek, S., & Smaldino, S. (2019). *Teaching and learning at a distance: Foundations of distance education.* Charlotte, NC: Information Age Publishing.

Swan, K. (2003). Learning effectiveness online: What the research tells us. *Elements of Quality Online Education, Practice and Direction, 4*(1), 13–47.

2

Understanding Online Education Environments

The Landscape, Where We Are, and Where We Want to Be

Edward Gonzalez

When it comes to online learning, I like to say, "you don't know what you don't know." For this chapter, we're probably starting at whatever the antecedent of that statement is. Before you learn, explore, or even dip your toe into the online teaching world, you need to know the lay of the land. This chapter is going to give you a survey of the online learning world and many of the tools, the current state of online learning, and a potential scenario for our collective aspirations.

Learning Management Systems and Instructional Content Platforms

When getting ready for a new school year the two things you worry about most are preparing the classroom and your curriculum. In an online setting, these two topics get the mandatory academic name with the accompanying acronym. I'm not going to drown you with new acronyms but for this chapter, you will need LMS and ICP. If at any point you forget their purpose, just remember that the learning management system (LMS) is the online classroom and instructional content platforms (ICP) are the curriculum replacing your books.

The typical LMS is an online platform that houses all of your digital learning needs. Within an LMS you should be able to enroll students, grade, take attendance, send messages, have discussions, and use a variety of extensions and third-party applications to enrich the learning environment. If you took online classes in college, chances are you have experience with Blackboard or Canvas. In the K-12 level, you may have also used Canvas, Schoology, or Google Classroom (which is pretty close to a full LMS system).

An ICP is almost an entirely closed ecosystem that does not integrate other software programs but may be integrated into an LMS. Wait a second, what? If Google Classroom is meant to be a digital classroom, an ICP would probably provide the content replacing a textbook. Let's consider the following online software such as NewsELA, where students can read current news articles that are leveled by Lexile and which includes quizzes and allows teachers to enroll students in a class. What makes this an ICP is that you absolutely can't import another application into NewsELA or have kids collaborate with each other. Compare this to Google Classroom, where you can import NewsELA into the LMS and keep track of your students from one location. The concepts might still be foggy, but as you see the functions of the tools, their purpose becomes clearer.

Blackboard, Canvas, and Schoology (BCS)

There are plenty of LMS systems available but I'm only going to talk about Blackboard, Canvas, and Schoology (BCS) because they serve well to illustrate the functions of an LMS. I discuss Google Classroom separately because it functions in a different way than the traditional LMS. If you have any experience with BCS, you may remember that awesome and dynamic online educator who brought your course to life! Or you might remember that totally disconnected feeling where it felt like you were walking along a desert trail with nobody in sight.

When you take a course in BCS, the experience is designed to be primarily independent. You can enroll in the course and proceed down that path at your own pace, which might be why you took an online course in the first place. Consider that many higher education students work, take care of families, etc. In a K-12 setting, you may have been in an online school or your school transitioned to online learning in a once-in-a-lifetime pandemic emergency. BCS allows students to take a course on their own time rather than spending a set time on campus.

Within BCS there are a variety of tools that can facilitate a more dynamic environment. The instructor can show achievements, create blogs, assign groups, proctor exams, and create wikis, among many more features. Notice that most of these tools are *asynchronous*, meaning that students will do the work on their own time and not at a set time.

BCS include robust grade books, technical customization features, and an ability to embed code from third-party software to integrate dynamic content. Within these LMS platforms, you can customize how the pages are presented and formatted. Consider BCS to be like a blank canvas that accepts all types of wet and dry media. You can paint, splatter, and splash with anything you want.

Google Classroom

If Blackboard, Canvas, and Schoology are like a blank canvas open to any tools, Google Classroom only allows you to paint with its brushes and pre-approved paints. The caveat is that while the traditional LMS is designed for asynchronous and independent learning, Google Classroom is designed to augment the classroom experience. As an extension to synchronous classroom learning, Google Classroom tends to do very well in promoting real-time learning within a simple platform.

Google Classroom is very similar to an LMS but is focused on G Suite applications (Google Docs, Google Sheets, Google Slides, etc.). As the platform evolves, Google Classroom is integrating many third-party applications directly into its system. For example, you can easily integrate NewsELA, Freckle, and Aeries into Google Classroom to make it easier to distribute assignments across different platforms. Consider Google Classroom to be a type of "command center" that can supplement a synchronous experience rather than totally replace it.

While the traditional LMS has multiple areas of navigation, Google Classroom is centered on the classroom "stream" where all assignments, discussions, and content are collected. This is very simple and intuitive for younger students to use, but does not provide the same robust organizational features of the larger LMS platforms.

The main draw of Google Classroom is that it is built for the G Suite ecosystem. This means that all of the G Suite tools easily integrate within Google Classroom at the push of a button, making it easier for the student and the teacher. By using G Suite, the user can access a variety of tools from a single account. What are these "tools" I speak of? Glad you asked, and on to the next section.

Tools

In order to understand how the variety of online tools work, it is important to recognize the majority are in some ways an update or remake of the tools of yesteryear, but now the far majority of these tools can be accessed from a web browser. Anybody who used a computer at some point in their education has worked with digital office tools like documents, spreadsheets, presentation software, and maybe computer-science-based programs for coding. The majority of the new fancy tools available are still fashioned on those same concepts. Within this section, I'm going to break down some of these updated concepts and provide examples of these types of new programs. Every tool mentioned in the following subsections is available on a website browser.

Google Drive and Microsoft Office

The current standard in educational office tools is set by Google and Microsoft. Google Drive and Microsoft Office provide access to documents, spreadsheets, presentation software, and various

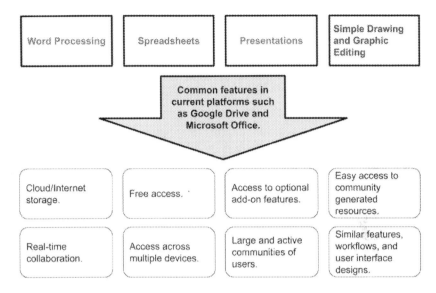

FIGURE 2.1 Updates to traditional office productivity software.

Source: Edward Gonzalez © 2020

other programs from a cloud-based service (Figure 2.1). In this way, you can easily access all of your files from any device with the capability to download their respective apps. For example, if you write a document on a Google Document within your computer browser you can edit that exact same document on your phone. This type of functionality is conducive for collaborating with others because you and your coworkers or students can all be writing and editing the same document from different locations.

Assessment

There are a variety of tools that act like traditional assessments where a student can access the quiz, proceed at their own pace, and then submit the quiz. Within Google Forms, you can design multiple-choice, short response, and Likert-style questions. Most programs also offer features where quizzes can include diverse media such as video, drawings, and images.

Synchronous quizzes can be facilitated in real-time by teachers. Online websites like Quizizz, Kahoot!, and Socrative have varying levels of free features that can be tailored for the specific needs of a learning environment. Kids typically rant and rave about the engagement of a program like Kahoot! where students compete within an assessment. The website Quizizz offers the same engagement features but takes the organizational aspect to another level by giving teachers the opportunity to save the scores with handy spreadsheets. The website Socrative takes on a much more academic feeling than Quizizz while allowing teachers to create assessments with a variety of delivery modes.

Presentation Software

Gone are the days of clicking away at dull presentations. You can still share presentations to be viewed asynchronously, but the interactive features for synchronous lessons provide different tools for student engagement. Many of the presentation programs also grant access to a vast library of user-generated presentations that users can remix for their own purposes. The diverse features available on presentation software platforms give educators the ability to embed video, incorporate animation, check for understanding in real-time, and collaborate with the viewers (Figure 2.2).

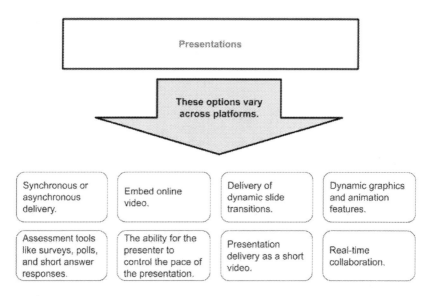

FIGURE 2.2 Updated features of modern presentation software and websites.

Source: Edward Gonzalez © 2020

Dynamic Visuals

Some presentation software simply jazz-up the traditional slide-show format. For example, websites like Prezi create a dynamic presentation that functions exactly like a PowerPoint, but uses unique transitions to whisk away the viewers. This type of software delivers on the "wow" factor but does not add functional differences or improvements.

Synchronous Engagement

Websites like Nearpod and Pear Deck break up the traditional lecture format by adding interactive features that can be facilitated and controlled by the presenter. Consider that within a traditional presentation, the user can proceed at will and on their own time. With software such as Nearpod and Pear Deck, the presenter has total control of the lecture just as they would in a traditional classroom.

Interactive presentation tools break up traditional presentations with features such as polls, surveys, and questions. This helps the presenter check for understanding in real time. Depending on the platform you can include 3D content, audio, video, and custom animations.

Video Presentations

The emergence of video as a medium for presentations has happened rapidly and broken open the possibility for sharing information in unique ways. Furthermore, access to these tools has rapidly evolved to the point where you can easily shoot and create high-quality video from your phone. Over the past few years, I have seen students take advantage of these applications to create unique project submissions. Another area of innovation within the realm of video production is animation-presentation websites. Programs such as Powtoon allow the user to create high-quality animations using a very simple interface. The added benefit is that videos can be shared on YouTube or social media and give students an audience they would not reach with a traditional pencil and paper.

Computer Science and Design Platforms

Perhaps the most innovative developments in the online learning environment are taking place within the realm of computer science (CS) and design tools. K-12 students now have a wide array of tools to begin learning CS and develop original content that can be shared on the internet. In previous generations, CS and design tools were more commonly found in elective courses for older students or special learning environments for younger students. Today, CS and design software tools have branched out to include such features as child-friendly block coding, 3D modeling tools, and VR development (Figure 2.3).

One of the older CS online platforms is Scratch, where the user can learn the foundational aspects of programming through visual programming. Other established CS platforms include Code.org and Khan Academy, which go further by providing tutorials and peer-based assessment on computer science languages like HTML, CSS, and SQL.

3D modeling within a web browser has evolved to the point where even young elementary students can design models with

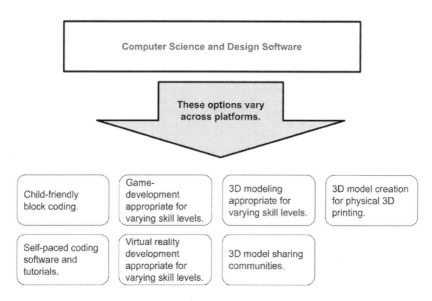

FIGURE 2.3 Modern computer science and development software.

Source: Edward Gonzalez © 2020

a relatively low barrier to learning how to manipulate the tools. Online websites such as TinkerCAD give students the opportunity to create their own libraries of 3D models or redesign models from a library of user-created models. More advanced software such as SketchUp includes robust tools to create designs that can be used in creating formal architectural designs. One of the defining features of these 3D modeling platforms is that students can export these designs and print them with 3D.

Where We Are

We've covered the landscape of online learning spaces and in this section, we will now describe the state of digital learning environments (immediately preceding the 2020 pandemic), access to these learning environments, and the potential of online learning. As of the 2020 pandemic, new teacher maxims emerged such as "the pandemic has brought to light equity issues." This phrase can be framed by the equity of access to digital devices, access to high-speed internet, and equity of technology-based instruction.

Access to Devices

It is important to first understand how students were accessing online environments leading up to the 2020 pandemic. In 2014 teens reported being online "almost constantly" at a rate of 24%; by 2018 that number rose to 45% (PEW, 2018a). This access is made possible considering that 95% of teens report having access to a smartphone and 88% claim they have access to a home computer (PEW, 2018a). These numbers vary across economic and demographic populations with white teens reporting access to desktops at a rate of 90%, Black teens at 89%, and Hispanic students at 82%, however, families that make less than $30,000 per year report 75% access to a home computer, compared to 96% of families that make $75,000 or more (PEW, 2018a).

The age and type of device also have an impact on whether or not it can be used for instruction. For example, a student may have access to a device but the device might not be able to access a particular educational application. In my own personal experience, the speed and performance of the device will also have a major impact on a student's and teacher's experience and their ability to work effectively.

Access to High-Speed Internet

Where you live in America has a big impact on your access to the internet. In a 2018 survey, the Pew Research Center reports that 13% of urban residents had a major problem with access to high-speed internet, compared to 24% of rural residents. This translates over to student access, as a survey on teens in 2018 reported that 13% of white students, 25% of Black students, and 17% of Hispanic students were "unable to complete homework because of lack of a reliable computer or internet connection" (PEW, 2018b). Socioeconomic status also exacerbates this divide as the same study showed that only 9% of students in families that make $75,000 or more report this problem, compared to 24% of students whose families earn less than $30,000.

Access to Quality Digital Instruction

Apart from access to devices and high-speed internet, under-served students also lack access to equitable instructional experience with digital tools. In a literature review on the use of technology by underserved students, Zielezinski and Darling-Hammond (2016) found that schools with minority students in a low socioeconomic setting consistently used technology to provide facts-based drill and practice learning activities, despite the fact that research shows those same groups of students perform much better when the technology is used to promote higher-order thinking skills. Furthermore, this same study showed that more interactive and critical thinking tech-nology-based lessons also improved the learning outcomes for at-risk students.

Where We Want to Be

My grad students were interviewing high-school-aged students around the world. In almost every case, what we heard was young people had a richer intellectual and creative life outside of school than inside it, that the things they learned from and the things they cared about were things they did after the school day was over. Jenkins (2013)

Kids are bringing their own dynamic skills and knowledge to 21st century digital tools, but when they enter a school campus, we are asking them to accept the academic and learning goals of our own system. Part of the reason is that technology has not changed the structures of schooling but merely changed the delivery of the content. The 2020 pandemic has managed to finally change these structures of schooling, but as a field how will we respond to these changes? Will we use the same curriculum and pedagogy but upload it in a digital format?

In a study on technology integration, Cuban (2018) reports that most teachers he interviewed reported technology increased their own productivity and freed them up to deliver better-individualized instruction. There is a need to assess whether we are using technology to make the life of educators easier or to provide new and exciting opportunities of inquiry for children. If you replace a hand-written essay with a digital essay, expect the same achievement gaps you had in the physical learning space. If you replace a ten-problem math quiz with a digital quiz that includes a YouTube video, expect the same achievement gaps you had in the physical learning space. The tools shouldn't only serve to make the teacher more efficient, they should serve the needs and the interests of the students.

So how should students be learning in online environments? You need the right balance of guidance, instruction, and inquiry. Students benefit from digital collaboration, inquiry-based learning, and the opportunity to share their learning in different ways (Zielezinski & Darling-Hammond, 2016). If the assignments and projects you are creating would not be inquiry-based, provide critical thinking opportunities, and promote collaboration in a physical setting, then those same assignments would not recreate those experiences in a digital setting.

Suggested Projects for Online 21st-Century Learning Environments

Wikis

A wiki is a crowdsourced website where multiple users collaborate to create a unified project. You can use a free platform like Google Sites to create a class website and assign students an individual page. Consider the age-old 3rd-grade classic "animal report" where kids create an individual report and share it in front of the class. You can update this project to be a class-wide animal website where each student shares their report along with images and videos.

Documentaries

Give students multiple options for sharing their learning. Rather than creating an essay or presentation, have the students create a script and short video. Middle school teacher Cattrice Toles has her students interview adults as part of a project for Black History Month and then shares the video with her school. Within this project, students create the interview questions, select the adults they will interview, and then edit the footage for an authentic audience.

Placed-Based Learning

Give students a task that requires them to solve a local problem. Third-grade teacher Bethany Gonzales has her students design a play structure that they will then promote within a video commercial. The students design, sketch, and then 3D model their project in TinkerCAD before creating a video with Screencastify where they pitch their project to the community.

Problem-Based Learning

Elementary teachers Valerie Perez, Jesus Huerta, and Paul Gordon all use 3D modeling with online software to promote critical thinking and build empathy with students. Valerie and Jesus have students design and create prosthetic models as part of their curriculum. When the 2020 pandemic began, it was these types of learning experiences that prompted one of Paul's students to begin making mask shields for local first responders.

Portfolios and Blogs

One of the most powerful ways to document learning is with a portfolio or blog. Consider that most assignments are only seen by the teacher and student, but within a portfolio or blog, a student can share their work with approved viewers or come back and revisit their own work later. A portfolio or blog can include artwork, videos, images, and journals. Depending on the website you select, there are always safety features to protect students online and keep students within a safe and private ecosystem. If students are using G Suite, they can use a Google Site as a portfolio and keep the settings restricted to specific users.

References

Cuban, L. (2018). *The flight of a butterfly or the path of a bullet? Using technology to transform teaching and learning.* Cambridge, MA: Harvard Education Press.

Edutopia. (2013, May 7). Henry Jenkins on participatory culture (Big Thinker Series). *YouTube.* Retrieved from https://youtu. be/1gPm-c1wRsQ

Pew Research Center. (2018a, May). *Teens, social media & technology 2018.*

Pew Research Center. (2018b, May). *What unites and divides urban, suburban and rural communities.*

Zielezinski, M. B., & Darling-Hammond, L. (2016). *Promising practices: A literature review of technology use by underserved students.* Stanford, CA: Stanford Center for Opportunity Policy in Education.

3

What If You Had a Second Teacher Brain?

Josh Harris

Introduction

What do Tom Brady, Serena Williams, Michael Jordan, and Megan Rapinoe have in common, other than being among the best in their respective sports? Among the things that they have in common is that no matter how far they have progressed in their career or their skills, they always had a coach. This was critical because the sports they all play continue to evolve and change over time. They have always had somebody who was an expert that could observe, help, guide, and provide feedback. Their coaches are a second set of eyes and ears and most importantly a second brain to help them learn, grow, improve, and also to help them anticipate what is coming. Their coaches are a person they trust to help them get better and anticipate their future needs. Their coaches are invaluable to them . . . and they never had to be coached on how to play through a pandemic over the internet.

After our first couple years as a classroom teacher, this concept of having a coach to help us keep honing our craft becomes foreign. Oftentimes the only setting in which there is another adult in our room is if we are being evaluated or observed by outside consultants who are really there to find fault and tell us what we're not doing well enough—also known as "providing accountability." This has bred a natural mistrust by classroom teachers around the idea of another adult being in the room whose whole job is to "help them get better."

Having a coach, no matter what the circumstances, is always a good idea. However, in the time of pandemics and reinventing education in the midst of a crisis, having a coach or a specialist to help you can make a world of difference. Even if we were used to working with some sort of educational coach before the pandemic, working with one during it is not easy. If you've never utilized some sort of educational coach before, getting to know one and forming a trusting relationship to be able to start utilizing one remotely is an even bigger challenge. In this chapter we will take a look at what you can do to facilitate building that trust with your coach and how to better work with them.

But of course in education, we cannot simply refer to anyone in this role as "coaches." On the west coast, we refer to them as teachers on special assignment, or TOSAs. Coming from California I have learned that not every part of the United States uses this term; however, the role and the job itself does exist in many places. When it involves teachers using technology more effectively to teach, the role has many names. It's referred to as an educational technology specialist, or instructional technology integrationist, or something similar. I have even heard "backpack leader" when the role is related to technology. In many school districts in California and across the country there are TOSAs in virtually every subject matter taught. Sometimes they are organized by grade level. For my purposes I will refer to them as EdTech TOSAs, or simply TOSAs. Some of the ideas here will apply to any sort of educational coach no matter what their title or area of expertise.

Many teachers and administrators are new to working with TOSAs. In some states there is very high suspicion amongst teachers and teacher associations of TOSAs. In other states they're just new and people are not sure what to make of them. For the EdTech TOSAs this is complicated by the idea that their job title might obscure some things about them, and people make assumptions about their association with the IT department. So let's start by saying what they are and what they aren't.

If I Can Understand It, Then I Can Trust It

What a TOSA Is

First and foremost, a TOSA is a TEACHER, hence the T at the beginning of that acronym. They are teachers whose whole professional purpose is to help and support classroom teachers. In the case of an EdTech TOSA there is often a struggle to clarify the difference between them and IT to teachers, especially if the role of the person is unfamiliar to the teachers and administrators they serve. When I became a TOSA myself I had been in education as a paraprofessional working with mainstreamed deaf students and as a middle school teacher for over 14 years. I had excelled in my craft and at using technology, and was considered a model teacher (there's evidence on YouTube). In most places the qualifications to become a TOSA require five years of classroom teacher experience as a minimum—the fewest I have seen is three. Most of the time, in my experience, these are exceptional teachers who have to be lured out of the classroom and into serving teachers instead of students directly.

What a TOSA Is Not

Let's just come out and say a few things. First, a TOSA is not a pseudo administrator, nor an administration spy. In many cases they are guilty by association and/or proximity. In my experience as an EdTech TOSA and with the team I lead now, TOSAs are led by a director or other district-level administrator. This tends to make classroom teachers view them as a "district/central office (DO/CO) person." Most of the time TOSAs do not have a place to work at school sites, so when they are not directly supporting teachers (at your school site; they often have several to support) they tend to work in the DO, casting more suspicion on them as some sort of spy. They are not reporting on teachers to administrators. The reality is that many of them still have their classroom teacher hearts and do their level best to bring the voice of the classroom teacher into the discussions with district leadership.

Second, they aren't failed teachers who the district just wanted to move away from kids. A thing you find out working with teachers and administrators from across the country is that we all assume our experience in education—and I mean every aspect, from day-to-day to community and culture—works for everyone else in our job the same way it works for us. NOT TRUE! I've worked in three different California school districts as a paraprofessional, a classroom teacher, TOSA, and an administrator, and while there certainly were commonalities, a lot more was local than I suspected ahead of time. I have worked with teachers and schools in about a dozen states and one province in Canada, and the differences are even wider on that scale. Which is all a caution against universalizing your experience. But here is a reality: in many regions across the nation this title or even class of teacher support comes with a lot of baggage. Some of these are very local and related to the history of a specific district, in other cases, it is true for a whole region. If you live in a place where TOSA is a dirty word, I encourage you to keep in mind there are places where we couldn't live without them. You may not find any at your site or in your district, but that doesn't mean you won't find amazing ones as you build your PLN (see Chapter 11 for more about that).

Why People Become TOSAs

Most of the TOSAs I know leave the classroom because they feel a drive they didn't start their career with—the drive to support and grow their fellow teachers. I know this was true for me and it remains true for me even as I have gone on to become an administrator. I have worked and networked with TOSAs from at least 20 states and the vast majority of them have this idea of serving teachers and (through those teachers) students for the greater good. Once many of us got to the TOSA role we found that we learned even more about teaching. If you think about it, when was the last time you really got a chance to watch other teachers work? A TOSA's whole job is to be there side by side with teachers, seeing what they are doing and sharing the experiences they've gleaned from other teachers with you. TOSAs learn a ton about teaching and real-world best practices because they get into more classrooms than just about anyone, including most principals. Becoming a TOSA is humbling. We end up learning how much we still have to learn about teaching, which redoubles most TOSAs drive to share and facilitate the growth of their colleagues.

Another common theme amongst TOSAs is, "I had to figure this out on my own; I am going to make sure other teachers don't have to." If you became a teacher to emulate your favorite one, or to be the amazing teacher you never had, you can understand this feeling. Specific to EdTech TOSAs is the enthusiasm of sharing, "OMG! This is so cool!" when it comes to technology—not technology for its own sake, but to see what kids and teachers can *create* with it. And I have to say I don't know a single TOSA who left the classroom to "get away from kids." In fact, as I said before, it's often hard to convince good teachers who also have the potential to be great TOSAs (not the same skill set) to leave the classroom because just like you, they *love* kids. If you know a TOSA who is always trying to get into your class, view that as a compliment. They want to be in your class because you make it a wonderful place and they want to be around your students—they miss it too.

The elephant in the room here is the idea that TOSAs are administrators-to-be. The real reason they go off to work at the DO is because they think it's a fast track to administrator, right? Wrong. Many TOSAs, at the start of their time in that role, will tell you that they have no intention of going into administration, and their time at the DO affirms this. Others start off that way only to find themselves as an administrator several years later. They were sincere when they said it, but time in the TOSA role might grow or change your perspective in unexpected ways. This is really similar to the drive to make sure that no one has to have the same difficult, rocky path as teachers did when they first left the classroom to become a TOSA. For me, as for many other administrators like me, the same impulse that drove me to make things easier for teachers then drove me to build a department where I could grow TOSAs. Some administrators who come up through the TOSA path skip being a site principal. This lends itself to keeping a lens that is all about growing teachers and responsive professional development.

The Work of a TOSA

What do TOSAs do all day anyway? Most TOSAs are assigned to multiple school sites, so it can be very tempting, since we rarely see them, to assume that they are in the district office sitting in front of a computer all day. This is rarely the case, and when it is the case and they seem to be on Facebook, Twitter, and YouTube all day, that's still work—especially for an EdTech TOSA. When we look at the work of TOSAs, we find that they have three core functions.

First, they are professional learners. Their goal is to drive pedagogy by being able to answer every single one of your questions in their area of expertise. They want to make sure they either have the answer on hand, or that they are well-versed enough with reliable experts and resources that they can look it up quickly for you—saving you time. They have to keep up with the state of the art in their area of expertise as well as keeping their teaching skills sharp. This may involve things that don't seem like work. Working in educational technology generally means that you need to be connected with people who don't work in your school district. Social media and networking are key to this effort, including YouTube, Facebook, Twitter, and various other platforms. The TOSA isn't wasting time, they are learning from others in their field—because the state of the art of EdTech changes so fast and other educators come up with innovative practices so fast that they feel like they MUST keep up with it, so you don't have to. Your EdTech TOSA might be a Google for Education Certified Innovator (GEI or GCI), Coach (GCC), or Trainer (GCT); they might be an Apple Distinguished Educator (ADE), or a Microsoft Innovative Educator Expert (MIEE). These all offer their own semi-exclusive PLNs that give them access to another community and set of resources and experts to draw upon.

Second, they need to take that professional learning, that "state of the art" information that they learn, and make it accessible and digestible to you. Just like lesson planning, building professional development materials takes time and TOSAs do not have the luxury of adopted curriculum or websites like Teachers Pay Teachers; there is no "TOSAs Pay TOSAs," and in the case of technology, something a TOSA built only a month ago could need major updates. (This is why they spend a ton of time networking, looking to borrow materials others have already made; fortunately, there is a strong "share and share alike" ethic in the EdTech world.) This might look like sitting in front of computers in their office for hours building resources like handouts, slide decks, newsletters, or websites. This might look like sitting with you or your grade level colleagues lesson planning, and then the follow-up co-teaching. It can take the form of one-on-one help with a teacher. Sometimes it means planning professional development (PD) based on a needs assessment done by a principal. But the overall theme of this work is taking the massive rushing river of EdTech and turning it into a small, drinkable glass of water for you that helps make your teaching, not just your tool use, better.

Third, there is the infamous phrase, "other duties as assigned." This can be such a grab bag or assortment of tasks that it's difficult to say what similarities there might be across the board. For the most part, it's usually tasks that facilitate or support the first two core functions. If we're going to hold a workshop for people somebody's got to reserve the facilities, order the water, and maybe pick up goodies for the teachers. It might mean sitting with folks from the curriculum and instruction department, co-developing their PD so that technology is integrated with the teaching practices and curricular content from the beginning, in essence trying to "bake the EdTech right in" so that it's not an incompatible, meaningless, afterthought to a new piece of training. It might be sitting in meetings with IT explaining why something that seems simple to them will be much more complicated when the technology rubber hits the classroom road or helping them understand why teachers need something they've requested. It might be helping put together a Google form survey for directors or assistant superintendents. It might mean filling in for a teacher when someone has fallen ill at the last minute and a principal needs help. It might mean setting up a Zoom for a school board meeting. It might mean putting on a student film festival for the whole district on short notice because they are the one who goes to all the sites and knows how to do video editing. Some of these things are within their scope and some of them are not . . . the downside of being an educational technology "guru" is that you get tagged in to do a lot of tasks simply because you have the skills, not because they are in your job description. Just know that most of us like to keep in mind, and to remind those around us, that our primary responsibility is to serve and support teachers.

How to Build Trust With Your TOSA

It goes without saying that the work of a TOSA absolutely depends on relationships. More specifically, that relationship has to be built on trust even more than collegiality. We know that for you as a classroom teacher to welcome in another adult and do all the things described in the opening of this chapter, you have to trust we have your best interest at heart and will care about you as a professional and as a person. When there is a lack of trust a TOSA will not be effective; you can ask any academic or educational coach in any field anywhere in the United States and they will echo this. Think of it as similar to your relationships with your students. At the beginning of school year, or when a student first enrolls mid-year, there is always that tentative "getting to know you" phase. This is when you as a teacher and they as a student should share your personalities but also learn to trust each other. The teacher begins to trust that the student actually wants to learn and to be there and will cooperate in the classroom culture and community. The student learns that the teacher will care for them, safeguard them, and wants them to grow as a learner and a whole person. The student can continue to learn once trust is established. The deeper the trust the deeper the learning. The same thing is true in athletics. Professional athletes often put their safety and their physical body on the line for their jobs. To do their jobs better and more effectively they put a large amount of trust for their physical as well as their psychological safety in their coaches.

This is no different for a TOSA. For them to succeed with you, you must trust each other.

There are a whole host of things well trained TOSAs and other instructional coaches should do to start building trust with you. But this chapter is not for them, this chapter is for you—the classroom teacher. It is highly unlikely that you took a class during your credentialing process and titled "how to build trust with your TOSA," so let's talk about a few ways to do that now. Some of this is not going to be that different from how you build trust with any other colleague or fellow classroom teacher. But at the heart of these ideas is the concept of vulnerability and taking risks.

An obvious commonality between you and any instructional coach you might work with is that you both work at least in the same school district, if not the same school. So obviously, talking generally about work is perfectly fine. Don't feel like you have to stick to pleasantries and don't feel shy about asking questions, even if they seem off topic. If your TOSA is assigned to several schools at the same time, they may have a different perspective or some different information than you will, having been only at your one school site. During my time as a TOSA, I discovered how many teachers just needed somebody to vent to. It seemed like there was actually some safety for them in venting to somebody who was not assigned to their school site. Also, don't worry about being perceived as negative. Many TOSAs consider themselves advocates for teachers. When you vent to them and they hear the same thing from multiple teachers they tend to pass that up the chain, especially if technology or other curricular rollouts are not going as planned or as advertised.

Another way we get to know people is to work on something together. This way, we see who they are, how they work, and we can learn to trust them. It helps to have a common goal or a project. In this case if you can think of some small task that you need a collaborator for, even if it's just another set of eyes or hands, that is a great initial task to work with your TOSA on. It gives you both the opportunity to see how the other one works and to get to know each other's communication styles. Additionally, this has the added benefit of getting something done that you wanted to get done anyway. Most of us in EdTech believe in the motto of #BetterTogether. In addition to small collaborative projects, there may be times when it's okay to ask your TOSA to take something small off of your plate. While you should never treat them as your technology secretary (techretary), occasionally there are one-off items using technology that your TOSA can do much faster, and as long as you don't come to rely on them for that, it is another way to build trust.

Lastly, just as we like to be judged on our own merits, remember that others at your school site or in your school district might have had experience with your specific TOSA or with coaches in general and may have opinions. This is a plan to ignore the gossip, take a chance, and decide for yourself. You never know what someone else's impressions are going to be, or why they decided something.

All of the work and practice above can be complicated and very human in a face-to-face environment. If you add in the factors related to working through distance learning and remote instruction, all of this becomes that much more complicated. How do you build trust when you can't work side by side? How can you be sure that if you vent to your TOSA over a video call there isn't someone who will accidentally overhear? By the time you're reading this, you've probably already gone through some version of distance learning and encountered all these complications, stressors, and frustrations, making it harder to be aware of and mitigate your own affective filter. If you have to continue or establish a coaching relationship with any support provider during distance learning, the best thing to keep in mind is to use the clearest communication possible. If you've ever taught writing to students and you find yourself saying things like "write it as though the person has no context," that is a great piece of advice here. It's definitely better to over clarify, be very specific, and use all the tools at your disposal. Also, don't be shy about being clear if you prefer a certain method of communication, and keep in mind that while you may not feel camera-ready, video calling remains the best way to really get a feel for somebody's human context when you can't be in the same room with them.

Your Second Teacher Brain—How to Use This Tool

What if Google and Alexa had a baby that became a teacher? And what if that "Googlexa" was your colleague? You could ask it for all kinds of help. This is how you can think of "using" your TOSA, or rather their skills and assistance. As we've seen, a TOSA is a support and a resource. Obviously, in their areas of expertise, and because of all the other areas their work takes them into, they can often answer other questions, or they know who to ask to get the best information. Most TOSAs can answer questions around curriculum and best practices, as well as policies and procedures as well. Think of your TOSAs as collaborating teachers who aren't assigned their own class. This means that they can co-plan and co-teach with you without having to worry about "making it work for their class too." It can be all about you and your kids when you ask to co-plan with a TOSA. Since they are not, and never should be, your evaluator, they are a low-risk observer in your classroom. If you would like to get feedback on your own practices and tendencies, a TOSA can be a great person to ask, knowing that it should stay between you and them; if you have concerns about confidentiality, spell that out with them ahead of time. Lastly, but definitely not least, because they are still, at their core, a teacher, they can be a great advocate for you. As mentioned earlier, they are an ear for many teachers in your same situation and will usually take a frequent or common concern or problem up the chain to try and advocate for improvement. Don't be afraid to ask them specifically to advocate for something you feel has some urgency.

Good Questions Get Good Answers

Did you notice that all the ways to work with a TOSA involved asking questions and getting answers? Just like Google and Alexa, your Googlexa support person needs good questions to render good support. However, you would be amazed how many full-grown, college-educated adults do not, in fact, ask good questions . . . or any questions at all. Think of a student who comes up to you holding something and says, "this isn't working right," or "I don't get it." Notice that neither of those are questions. Now think of all the counter questions you have to ask to figure out what isn't working for the student. Think about how many times the student responds with, "but I already tried that!" Now make that whole exchange happen in email, without pictures, with a variable time delay between each side's response. Sound fun?

Let's think about asking good questions, and dealing with solutions:

- Make sure you are actually asking a question, not making a statement. Just like the statement in the previous example, don't make your listener infer the question. "Zoom doesn't work for me" is not only a statement, it's so vague that the TOSA has to start at a really basic level to get anywhere useful. An important side note about asking questions (that are actually questions) when working in distance learning or remotely at all is to say this: pictures are good, annotated pictures are better, video is best (and video where you can screenshare is the ultimate). It can be so much more difficult to convey all the nuances of a question through email or text. Taking the time to use the right medium to ask the questions and have a discussion will pay down the road.

- This is *very* true for technology-based questions, but it's a good idea all around: if you're trying to solve a problem or correct something, state what you have already tried when you ask the question. This one is a real time saver.

- Be honest with yourself about the problem driving the question, and be open to the source of the problem not being what you are certain it is. It can be very tempting and easy to place the locus of the problem being on the technology, the circumstances, the adopted curriculum, or some group of people. This may not be where the problem lies. This by no means indicates that you are the problem—I've helped many teachers whose first assumption is always that they are doing it wrong. In addition to not being good self-care, it lets others off the hook incorrectly.

◆ Be willing to hammer your question into shape. Meaning, sometimes we need a thought partner who can talk through a question or problem with us, so that we ask the right question to get at the heart of the underlying problem.

◆ Try to keep your objective in mind; don't be married to a specific tool or process. If you are beholden to a specific tool or process, be honest about why, even if your answers aren't very strong. If you have decided ahead of time that you can only use a certain tool or do things a certain way, you are setting yourself up for frustration and disappointment. The tool you have already chosen may not do what you want at all or very well. Additionally, if you're closed off from a solution because it means learning something new or doing an unfamiliar attempt, you are limiting yourself and your solutions and potentially adding to your frustration long term.

◆ Persist in the face of failed attempts. This is something that we ask students to do, and it's number one of the eight mathematical practices, yet it can be hard. It can feel like we have failed or that the TOSA has, but we learn more from failure than success. Check out any number of videos on youcubed.org to hear Jo Boaler talk about how much more our brain grows when we address our failures (especially in math). If what you and the TOSA came up with doesn't work, revisit the solution, the implementation, and be willing to look at it again. This need for persistence and perseverance is why saving time in the early stages is key.

Negotiating Frustrations—Where the Trust Tires Hit the Complication Road

Lest you think that I have painted a flawless, rosy picture of how this collaboration, coaching, and support will go, make no mistake there will be frustrations and disagreements. However, the mark of open, growing professionals is that they can negotiate those frustrations and disagreements, learn from them, and build even deeper trust and relationships. So what are the parameters for negotiating these disagreements and frustrations?

For starters, as the teacher, the one receiving the support, the one calling on the expert help, you need to remember that it is perfectly acceptable to say, "I am not okay with this." When it comes down to it, you are going to be the one who has to put it all into practice. The TOSA serves to support you, not the other way around. (Do keep in mind that serving you is not the same as being your servant; that's an important distinction.) It may not feel comfortable to say that, but as the client, it is your responsibility to yourself and your students when you feel that way. It should go without saying that this needs to be done respectfully and professionally. However, you must also remember that it is the responsibility of the TOSA to grow and develop the teachers she serves. Just as it is your responsibility to say, "I am not okay with this," it is their responsibility to ask, "why aren't you?" You may not have an answer in the moment, but that's okay, talk it out with the TOSA. What isn't professional and shouldn't be accessible to the TOSA is if your answer basically comes down to, "I just don't wanna." We are adults, so we know all kinds of ways to mask and obfuscate "I just don't wanna," even to the point when we can hide from ourselves that that is what we are doing. An experienced, well-trained TOSA knows this. If they think they hear you saying, "I just don't wanna," be prepared for some questions. Remember these aren't attacks, or even doubts, they are just questions. The TOSA might be seeking to understand, or they may be going through coaching cycle questions to dig deeper; that's their job.

The TOSA isn't the only one who should be asking questions when things have hit a frustration or disagreement point. You should be asking questions too. It's far better to ask questions than it is to make assumptions. These assumptions can range from you guessing at the TOSA's motivations or goals, or suspicion around district actions and agendas. Turn your assumptions into questions—even blunt ones. By asking questions you give your TOSA an opportunity to be direct and honest with you. In my experience, they generally will be, even when they think you won't like the answers. The need for clarity, and clarity driven by honest and direct questions which are stated clearly, is even more critical when your collaboration and work with your TOSA is not face-to-face. If you are in a distance learning situation, regardless of the medium of communication, asking these questions is absolutely vital to building trust and the coaching relationship. Again, text is okay, pictures are better, video is best; a video call can go a long way towards clearing up misconceptions and talking through frustration and disagreement. We all know there is no tone in email. When we are texting someone, we can at least use emojis to help us convey tone, but that face to face is even more critical when there are complications.

Other times the complication has nothing to do with the TOSA and the teacher, but is a limitation that comes from outside the coaching relationship. This can and should be a unifying complication, a sort of "us against the world" situation. A primary example of this is when somebody who is the direct or indirect supervisor of either you or the TOSA says that whatever it is you're trying to do needs to stop for whatever reason. In this instance, it is probably best to huddle up and strategize. This is so situation dependent that it's hard to give clear guidelines; context matters. Since there are two of you, the chances are likely that you report to two different supervisors. There are plenty of times when the two of you can team up and try to get a green light from at least one of the supervisors. Then the one who said "yes" can appeal to the administrator who said "no." It's amazing how often understanding shifts on the part of the person giving the answer when a different voice asks the question. Other times there are just circumstances in the world that thwart us. These can be something like running past a deadline, or procedural hurdles that are prohibitive. These outside limitations could be related to funding or lack of resources. Again, this is an opportunity to come together and see what we can do with teamwork. But we must also accept that sometimes these outside circumstances cannot be overcome. When this is the case, blame is not helpful. Since working with or around these limitations can often mean an extra commitment of time, before one or the other person decides to commit to that, it is best to have a discussion. Make agreements on what you are both willing to do and to commit to in order to overcome these limitations. To reiterate what has already been said, trust and communication are keys to success here.

Frustrations can (and should) build trust and relationships. You have probably read or heard dozens of clichés about something like "in some languages, challenge and opportunity are the same word." It's true that those are clichés, and they can seem quite saccharine, but if we deal with frustrations and challenges in the right way, the clichés are true. Responding to frustrations and challenges with open and honest communication has already been covered. Overcoming or even just dealing with setbacks means that we are building our repertoire of common experiences with somebody. If you put together enough common experiences, we call that a relationship. If we can put all these things together into practice:

- ◆ asking good questions and accepting the solutions even when we didn't anticipate them,
- ◆ engaging in honest and clear communications even when we are not fully comfortable with the medium,
- ◆ refraining from making assumptions (good or bad) in favor of seeking information,
- ◆ being willing to collaborate through the frustrations, as opposed to avoiding them,
- ◆ embracing vulnerability and taking every chance we can to build trust, and
- ◆ remembering the grace and flexibility everyone needs when doing this if we can never meet face to face

. . . then we will build amazing relationships with the TOSAs whose professional goal is to help us be more skilled teachers, which will in turn benefit our students.

4

Don't Put the Digital Cart Before the Horse

Knikole Taylor

"You get a device! You get a device! You get a device!" These are the words I hear being yelled in my mind over and over in Oprah's voice as she hands out her favorite things. As I walk in classrooms to assist teachers with technology integration, I imagine the same spirit of giving is what took place as they were given technology in the same Oprah spirit to use in their classrooms. In the spirit of giving devices to teachers and students, I often see many teachers struggle with what to use on said devices. There are thousands of technology tools to use, so which should you choose? How do you know where to start? To be honest with you, it can be a lot. What we are really going to discuss is how to teach online without going crazy.

I'm going to let you in on a little secret about how to teach online without going crazy before we get started. The secret is that there is no secret. Teaching with technology is not a silver bullet. Good teaching is just good teaching. It's solid pedagogy combined with content and knowledge of your students. It's creating a clear roadmap from your learning standards to assessing the learning and crafting a plan to allow technology to help us.

After spending ten years in the classroom, I was an instructional coach for a number of years before entering into the world

Learning Standard(s)	
What should students know?	What should students be able to do?
Prior Knowledge	
Essential Question(s)	
Engage!	
Acquire	
Analyze	
Act	

Framework for Online Learning

of EdTech, and from the classroom to campus administration and later district administration, I have learned that good teaching is good teaching. When you strip everything to the bare bones, before you turn on any iPads or Chromebooks, you must have good pedagogy. We have to know our standards and our content along with how to get kids from point A to B to C. In this chapter, I will give you some tools to use and consider before you look at the tech pieces of your lesson. We will then discuss the necessary steps needed to be successful with online learning.

Content (Learning Standards)

Your first step to success is content. Content is what your students need to know. This encompasses your learning standards, or whatever students should know and be able to do. Dependent upon how learning standards are bundled, you may spend a couple of days on specific content, or it may take longer for an entire unit. However, the first step is looking at the standard and creating a learning plan. This will help you figure out how to get kids from where they are to where the standard says they need to be. I love the tools like I'm a techie, but we have to start here. What should kids know? What should they be able to do? We rely heavily on that state standard to set the pace for learning before identifying technology tools for the job.

Identify Your Content

Standard	What should students know and be able to do?
Solve real-world problems to find the whole given the part and percent, to find the part given the whole and the percent, and to find the percent given the part and the whole	• Solve problems • Find the whole when given the part and percent • Find the part when given the whole and percent • Find the percent when given the part and the whole

For example, the learning standard says students should solve real-world problems to find the whole given the part and percent, to find the part given the whole and the percent, and to find the percent given the part and the whole. *What does that even mean?* This is the question that we must answer first in order to have a clear understanding of what students should know and be able to do. Further examination of the standard shows that students should be able to find the whole, percent, and part of a number given different pieces of information.

Prior Knowledge

Next, we look at what kids learned before this lesson or before this grade level. What knowledge are they bringing with them? Having a clear understanding of the knowledge students should have *prior* to this lesson will help you plan for misconceptions. Did students learn these concepts last year? Is this concept new to them and unrelated to things they learned in previous years? Planning with this knowledge in mind allows you to set a course of action for success.

Essential Questions

After we know what they're supposed to know and what knowledge they bring with them, then we can establish our essential questions. Of course, these things don't have to be in this order. It just depends on how your brain works. I kind of like the questions because they give me a goal to work towards or an objective for students to master. This task could be open-ended or performance-based, and essential questions are going to rely heavily on the language or the vocabulary of the learning standard because that's how we're going to check to make sure that kids are actually getting exactly what it is they need.

Essential questions should elicit thinking. These are not simple yes or no questions. Essential questions push kids to critically think and this is really where we start to consider how we get the kids to utilize the Seven Cs of 21st-Century Learning: critical thinking, collaboration, creativity, cross-cultural understanding, communication, computing, and career and learning self-reliance.

Using the same learning standard, let's evaluate how we can turn simple questions into essential questions. Simple questions do not push students to communicate and elaborate on their answers. Essential questions allow students to synthesize their learning to share what they know.

Simple question	Essential question
Is 25% of 100 25?	How is percent related to fractions and decimals?
Should we use the percent or the decimal?	When and where might we need to know the percent or decimal equivalent of a number?
Is this solved correctly?	Explain the relationship between a whole, part, decimal, and percent.

Carefully crafted essential questions guide our instruction and push students to evaluate, create, and collaborate with their peers. Again, we rely heavily on the vocabulary of the standard because the standards outline the required vocabulary needed for content mastery. As I evaluate learning standards, I'm pulling the verbs right back out to ensure students are able to complete the expected actions of the standard. For example, if the standard says students should communicate, does it say that kids should explain, or does it say that kids should identify, because that's going to tell me how rigorous the lesson needs to be. I'm looking for activities that are aligned with the rigor, or learning verbs, of the standard. This will also allow me to better map out how the standard is going to be taught and evaluated.

We can capitalize on both local assessment data and classroom assessment data to learn what context will kids be evaluated over the standard. Lastly, we want to think about misconceptions. Data is always king here. Utilize data because data tells you what to do. As you plan, utilize the data not only to understand the needs of students but also to inform your own practices as a facilitator of learning. When I evaluate data as the teacher I'm looking at my data to see where I need to fix things also. What are my misconceptions? Perhaps I didn't teach the specificity of the learning standard, or maybe I chose a tool that did not meet the desired level of rigor. I also use data to be a reflective practitioner and plan for my mistakes, so even before I evaluate technology tools for teaching and learning, this is where I start to ensure that I know what kids need to know so I am able to meet their learning needs.

Engage!

Next, we're ready to engage! How will the students learn? Now that I know *what* students will learn, I am going to get them there. A good rule of thumb that I live by is that if I'm not engaged, I know the learners are not engaged. As the lesson designer, I identify an engaging lesson as a learning experience that meets the specificity and rigor of the learning standard in a meaningful way. As I am designing, I'm looking for opportunities to make the learning fun for the learner and fun for me to facilitate. How do I make the lesson something that kids would enjoy? There are many technology tools that do various things. However, it is important to select the correct tool for the job during your lesson.

Thinking about engagement and creating online spaces where kids want to talk to you and where kids want to talk to each other, we can sometimes put the cart before the horse, and simply grab the technology tool before evaluating how it will be used to help students master content.

If we are going to evaluate learning, you need a framework. Acquire, Analyze, Act is a simple three-part formative assessment system to evaluate student learning. During my first year as an EdTech coach, my teammates and I developed this system to support our teachers with an easy format to use technology to assess student learning.

First, you need to **Acquire**, or determine how you are going to get the data. The strategies listed in this chapter all provide different ways to evaluate student learning for free. Each one has a unique opportunity to evaluate the progress of student mastery.

Next, **Analyze** that data and determine how to make it useful. The only purpose in getting data is to get a plan together and act on it, which is why formative assessment data is an ongoing process that happens throughout the lesson cycle.

The last step is to **Act**, which could be differentiation, remediation, or extension. I feel like most of us have learned how to teach and plan for what happens when students don't understand. We automatically differentiate within high, low, and medium, and we think reteach and small group instruction. However, if you're going through this framework in practice and you're putting this framework in place and kids are learning, you need to be prepared for what happens when the kids actually understand, and planning for these next steps should be based on data.

The formative assessment cycle is ongoing during every class period from lesson to lesson and this is why we collect data. The formative assessment process is recurrent and helps us to meet the needs of students from the beginning of the lesson until they have demonstrated mastery. We want to constantly pivot and change to make plans in order to not only help our students, but also to remain informed of our own practices and our learning needs. A few examples of tools that help to inform teaching and learning are Kahoot!, Nearpod, and Google Forms. Along with providing multiple ways to assess learning, each one of these platforms provides its own data to help the teacher make an informed decision.

Each one of these tools has its own data output. After you ask a question you immediately have data that you can use to inform your next step or the next segment of your lesson so that you know what you need to do. This is why it's so important to spend the time on the content in step one, so that you know your goals for lesson mastery and have ample time to plan for student misconceptions. You are also able to craft a plan for what to do when kids don't know the content. I already know the knowledge that kids should bring to the table, so that's why it's so good to spend that time at the front, before selecting technology tools, which can also help to prevent you from putting the digital cart of tools before the learning horse. Once I actually know what kids need to know and be able to do, I'm able to find the appropriate tools to help them get there.

Google Classroom is a great tool we can use to act on data. Students can join multiple classrooms, and you can also differentiate by readiness level. I love Google Classroom because I can push out documents to specific students based on their learning needs.

HyperDocs are digital documents that encompass all of the components of a complete lesson cycle. They are created to provide a blended learning experience that centers student learning and serve as a great option for differentiation, extension, and remediation, or to meet the needs of all learners. To learn more about HyperDocs, visit https://hyperdocs.co/. There, you can learn about how to create your own HyperDocs and see examples of K-12 cross-curricular HyperDocs created by teachers from around the globe.

For example, you can use a HyperDoc to embed videos for reteach, or you can even embed those videos for choose-your-own-adventure based on how kids perform. They're also self-paced, so that's actually a good thing for students as well. HyperDocs and choice boards are also great tools to differentiate student support. You can add specific assignments and assign work to students based upon their needs.

When we think about our framework for online success, it's easy to plan for success. Taking the time to have a clear path to success for students enables us to align pedagogy, data, and engagement with technology tools for teaching and learning. Then, we are able to build up a community of learners that are engaged through purposeful interactive lessons.

5

Student Engagement in Both Synchronous and Asynchronous Online Learning

Susan Stewart

Making the shift to teaching online requires teachers to acquire an entirely new set of teaching skills. For most educators, the idea of teaching fully online was never a consideration to be prepared for. It certainly hasn't been a part of teacher preparation programs or professional development plans. In order for teachers to make this transition successfully, there is a need for a tremendous shift in instructional design that raises many questions.

How will students learn? Where will the new knowledge come from? How will they show us what they know?

Additional questions emerge in regards to student engagement. How can we promote meaningful engagement in this new, unfamiliar learning environment?

How do we know if they are with us when we can't see their faces in the chairs in front of us? How do we check for understanding? How do we know when to push a little further because some interest was sparked, and how do we know when to pull back and reteach because we just aren't there yet? And then what happens when students don't engage?

Teaching online means developing new ideas and practices around classroom management that focus on meaningful student engagement that goes beyond procedural compliance. Kids need reasons to be excited to engage in this learning environment and not just do what they are supposed to do because the teacher said so. To maximize the potential of online learning, opportunities for student engagement must be intentionally integrated into the learning plan.

Defining Terms

Synchronous engagement would be the kind of engagement during learning that happens with students and teachers working at the same time, on a common schedule. Students are typically following a prescribed pacing and path with shared learning timelines. During the emergency distance learning models in the 2020 COVID-19 crisis, synchronous learning has commonly referred to learning that happens live using one of the many video conferencing platforms. Teachers and students meet together, and students work on the content at the same time as other students.

On the other hand, asynchronous online learning refers to learning that occurs on students' own schedules. While there still may be shared expectations, timelines, and due dates, students work on their own. Teachers provide videos, resources, and assignments for students using Google Classroom, websites, or a learning management system (LMS).

What does meaningful engagement look like during online learning? For the purpose of this chapter, we will discuss engagement through the lens of both synchronous and asynchronous learning.

There are many factors that might impact the balance of the amount or proportion of synchronous and asynchronous learning that might happen in an online learning program. Some schools have limited the amount of video conferencing that teachers can use for synchronous learning, or even prohibited it. In some situations, schools use synchronous online time specifically as an opportunity to deliver lessons and direct instruction.

In other models, the synchronous time is set up to be open office hours, where students can stop in for assistance.

Whatever model your school might have in place, engagement will be a large contributing factor in the success of your online learning program.

Engaging Synchronous Online Classes—Meeting With Students

Many online platforms provide users the opportunity to hold virtual meetings. Some common tools include Google Meet, Zoom, Microsoft Teams, and WebEx. These platforms have many common features, including the potential to have users show themselves live through webcams and speak using device microphones. Having a live conversation and asking questions is a great start to engage with students who are not physically in our classrooms!

In most of these platforms, users have screen layout options that allow them to see one other user (typically the one who is speaking). This allows students to focus on the teacher who is giving live lesson or demonstration. Other layout options often give participants a chance to view multiple users at once. These grid-view or tiled-view layouts are useful for full class conversations. Students who have been isolated at home often appreciate the ability to engage with their peers virtually.

One important component of synchronous online learning in these video conferencing tools is that they provide an essential layer of human connection. Classes held synchronously are an opportunity to check in with students. Building rapport with students will help make synchronous learning more engaging. Don't be afraid to use a little more time than usual to chat and connect! If you're comfortable, share something from your home environment, perhaps a book, a pet, or a stuffed animal in your home that you wouldn't normally have a chance to share if you were working in the classroom. If students are comfortable, have them do the same. Ask about the kitten or little brother who keeps appearing on the screen. When students feel more connected to the learning environment, they will be more likely to engage.

Some of these video conferencing tools also provide the meeting creators with additional rights to monitor and moderate the meeting attendees. This might include the ability to mute a user's microphone, disable their camera in the meeting, or remove the user from the meeting completely. Teachers who hesitate to engage with students synchronously because of an unfamiliarity or fear of managing students in a virtual environment would greatly benefit from becoming familiar with those common features that can aid in virtual classroom management.

Additional features in these platforms often give participants the ability to use a chat or Q&A feature to ask questions or make statements during a synchronous lesson. These side chat features can be another powerful layer of engagement with online students. Students can ask questions in this text format and then the teacher can answer them live. Often, students use these chat tools and answer each other's questions, too. While having a backchannel of dialogue happening during instruction might seem like it could be a distraction, the ability for students to have that chat conversation is often a benefit. It allows for another authentic layer of engagement where students can process and share their learning.

Beyond the basic text-based interactions, some video conferencing tools have additional settings that allow students to engage through actions such as giving a thumbs up, raising a hand, or even offering applause or other visual/emoji-based interaction. It's important that teachers and students have an opportunity to become familiar with the basic functions, layouts, and engagement options of these platforms.

Once students are connected, teachers can hold class by speaking to students live and/or by presenting content by sharing materials on their screen. Screen-sharing is a common way that teachers explain and demonstrate content. Some teachers will use extensions or software to increase the size of their cursor. This acts as a visual support to students who are following along.

There are a variety of types of content that a teacher might share during a synchronous lesson. This could a be a website being shared as an explanation of walk-through of a topic or material. Some teachers prepare lesson slides using a variety of presentation tools, including PowerPoint, Google Slides, Smart Notebook files, and more. Teachers often use this presentation content as a focus point while they lecture on a topic. Having a pre-planned lesson in one of these presentation formats allows the teacher to pre-plan the lesson and have intentionality in the content flow. Using visuals, audio, clear images, and videos as a part of these lectures allows students to engage with the content visually while the teacher delivers the lecture or lesson.

Some teachers also teach these live, synchronous lessons by using physical books, papers, and whiteboards on camera to show examples as well as model concepts. Teachers will sometimes use document cameras to show work being completed. These might be the traditional document camera teachers have had in their classrooms. The emergency online learning crisis also saw many teachers creatively rigging up homemade document cameras using iPads, cell phones, and other mobile devices.

To improve lesson clarity and visibility, some teachers will use digital whiteboard tools to more clearly display writing during video conferences. This makes the content more accessible and engaging for the learners. Students can watch as the teacher writes a sentence, annotates text, or solves math problems. Some video conferencing software tools have embedded whiteboard functions. Some teachers will use other whiteboard tools to display content during a synchronous lesson. These include Google's Jamboard, Viewsonic's MyViewboard, and iPad apps including Explain Everything and Notability. To add an additional layer of engagement, some whiteboard apps can be used collaboratively. Students can be engaged in the lesson by participating with the task through the whiteboard app. An elementary teacher might use Jamboard to have students arrange letter cards during a phonics activity, or a secondary math teacher might use it to have students describe and explain the steps in solving an equation.

To facilitate these multiple learning windows during a synchronous lesson, many teachers find it helpful to use a second monitor or second device during the video conference lesson. This allows the teacher to display and engage with content on one screen, while still having the student videos and/or chat screen visible at the same time. The teacher can monitor the student engagement while continuing to teach. This also makes it easier for the students to offer visual engagement with a nod or "thumbs up" either physically or in the chat. An example of this might be when a teacher has demonstrated something that the students should complete in another window. Having students offer a "thumbs-up" or making a simple statement like "I'm back" is a quick way for the teacher to know when the students have completed the task and can move on.

In a synchronous lecture style format, interactive tools such as Pear Deck or Nearpod also provide an additional layer of engagement. Students can follow along with the lecture as it is delivered live. The tools provide multiple engagement points that are built into the software. This might be a text response, a drawing response, a multiple-choice question and many other options. As the teacher lectures, students view the teacher's slides. The teacher can pause their delivery for an intentional check for understanding (CFU) using the tool's interactive features. For example, a social studies teacher might be lecturing on a topic and pause to ask students a quick multiple-choice question to verify and reinforce understanding. An ELA teacher could pause the lesson to use a live engagement tool to have students make a prediction or offer an opinion on a text.

As teachers design engagement activities that occur during synchronous lessons, it's important to consider the needs and experience of the learners. Having students open new tabs might make them click away from the video conferencing software. Teachers should be mindful of this and make sure students have enough experience navigating between tabs in the online learning environment.

Synchronous Engagement—Formative Assessment and Checking for Understanding

Formative assessment is an effective way to monitor teaching and learning. In formative assessment, teachers take frequent measures of progress and use the information to adapt instruction. In traditional classrooms, teachers use a variety of formative assessment tools in the form of whiteboards, exit tickets, and quick writes before, during, or after a lesson.

Digital formative assessment tools offer teachers an opportunity to have instant feedback during a lesson. A benefit of doing this digitally is that student answers are often scored/tabulated automatically to provide instant results. Also, these online tools are often game-based, which increases student engagement. Many students are motivated by the music, graphics, and competition in these gamified checks for understanding. Some current popular digital formative assessment tools include Kahoot!, Quizizz, Formative, and Quizlet.

While many of these digital formative assessment tools have traditionally been used in the face-to-face classroom setting, many easily make the transition to a synchronous online learning environment. Teachers can run a live formative assessment as an opening, closing, or in the middle of a video-conference-based lesson to measure understanding of the content being taught or to be taught. Teachers can use the information that is instantly collected to reteach and refocus the current lesson, or as a way to plan for what comes next in instruction.

Synchronous learning is an important part of a remote learning plan. It's an effective way to bring students together to teach, reteach, and support students' individual learning needs. Through creative planning and intentional design, teachers can engage students and encourage active participation in synchronous learning.

Engaging With Asynchronous Online Lessons

When students access learning content in their own time without a teacher, that is often referred to as *asynchronous instruction*. The amount of synchronous and asynchronous instruction students have will vary according to policies and plans within a school district.

Designing engaging asynchronous learning requires thoughtful and intentional planning. It's essential that teachers consider student access and workflows in order to maximize engagement, effectiveness, and efficiency. Some considerations when design-ing any kind of blended or online learning program include:

> Where are the students? What are the students doing?
> Where is the teacher? What is the teacher doing?
> What is the content? Where will it be accessed?

Learning Models—What Are the Students Doing?

In some blended online learning models, a portion of the learn-ing and engagement is synchronous (either in person or online) and some is also asynchronous. An example of this could be when a teacher models a concept or idea during a live video conference, and then afterwards, students engage with addi-tional practice and activities independently. The teacher may also offer additional resources including links and videos that reinforce the concept that was shared in the live lesson. In this example, part of the learning is synchronous and part is asynchronous. Students have multiple ways to access and engage, which provides opportunities to better meet the needs of all students.

In a flipped online model, students engage with the content asynchronously first, and then synchronous learning time can be used for application and discussion. Teachers can also use the synchronous time for formative assessment and reteaching as needed to fill in what the students need to achieve profi-ciency. In some online learning programs, asynchronous lessons may be the only instructional format available to students. While it will look different from synchronous engagement, asynchronous online learning also offers many opportunities for student engagement.

Asynchronous instruction affords learners flexibility in their engagement schedule. When there isn't a set time when stu-dents are to be online for school, they can access the learning in a time that is most convenient and appropriate to their home lives. Because of a variety of levels of access and support in stu-dent homes, this flexibility is essential for maximizing student engagement.

Asynchronous Platforms—Accessing Content

In order to maximize student engagement in asynchronous learning, teachers should first make sure that students fully understand their online learning platform. Students should be well-versed in how to connect to and access their lessons. Building fluency and familiarity in navigation of the chosen online learning platform will help students find success in the asynchronous learning model.

One way to develop this familiarity is through the creation and/or curation of video tutorials specifically about how to access the platform. Video directions about how to access learning tasks are useful for many reasons. Recorded content offers the ability to watch and rewatch the videos to build up that fluency. Video tutorials can also help support parents who are supporting students in their home learning and might be completely unfamiliar with the digital learning environment.

Whatever platform is used, it's important to establish routines and use clear, consistent practices. Developing consistent expectations and routines will help students better engage with the online content. This clarity will also help parents who often have the role of supporting students during home learning. Teachers should develop routines and protocols around how the content is organized, managed, and delivered. Students should know exactly where to go to access and engage. Some examples of this might include having a weekly outline, lesson plan, or newsletter that keeps the learners updated on the expectations and goals. This could also be done with a weekly or daily video message from the teacher.

This clarity in instructional design should also include clear workflows and an understanding of how to submit or return completed assignments. Providing students with checklists or other means to self-monitor progress and engagement goals will help students develop independence and accountability for their own learning.

Some schools will provide teachers and students with a commercial learning management system (LMS). An LMS is a platform designed to house, deliver, and track online learning.

These systems provide a portal where students can engage with all aspects of their online learning. Many LMSs have built-in features to track and monitor student engagement.

Many schools use Google Classroom as the hub for asynchronous online learning. This tool is a part of the Google Suite for Education and is available for free to schools who have set up a GSuite domain. While commonly accepted as an effective tool for online learning, Google Classroom is not a full LMS. Combining Google Classroom with other applications from the Google Education Suite provides a wide variety of options for students to engage with the learning content.

Some schools' learning plans ask teachers to develop websites to house and share their online learning instructions and manage online content such as links and videos. In some circumstances, teachers communicate asynchronous learning expectations through email and other online communication apps.

Teaching Asynchronously With Engagement in Mind!

In asynchronous learning, the role of the teacher shifts. In place of teaching live lessons, the teacher prepares lessons for students to access independently. Teachers create and post assignments to the learning platform. This might include videos, presentations, writing prompts, online quizzes, and independent or collaborative student activities. Students complete each of these activities in their own time. To maximize student engagement, teachers should be sure to provide multiple options for students to access and apply the new learning. Embedding some choice in these learning paths will improve engagement as students appreciate the autonomy to select the learning activities themselves based on their own interests and learning style.

It's important to note that many of the tools used for synchronous engagement also have features that can be used asynchronously as well. The gamified quizzing applications mentioned previously typically have a "home" mode in addition to the live modes used in the synchronous environment. These can be assigned asynchronously in the learning platform as a way to increase engagement and check for understanding.

High-quality video lessons are often an important component of an asynchronous online learning program. Much of the instruction occurs this way. Students watch video lessons and then have opportunities to practice and apply the concept. Sometimes these videos are created locally, by the individual teacher or by specific teachers assigned to content creation for multiple classes or across the grade levels. Teachers who do deliver synchronous lessons can take advantage of the recording features that are embedded in the video conferencing software to record their live lessons to be accessed asynchronously. This will make the content available to students who weren't able to attend the live lesson.

Teachers can record their own video lessons using free screen recording tools such as Screencastify or Screencast-O-Matic or using the native screen recorder on an iPad. There are many other screen recording software options available commercially. Just as when planning live or synchronous lessons, teachers can design slides or other teaching materials to include as a part of the recorded lesson. Pre-recorded video lessons can be an engaging and equitable way for students to receive instruction. Students can access the videos in their own time. They can also rewind and rewatch the videos as necessary. Some LMSs have embedded features that track students' video viewing engagement. EdPuzzle is another tool that will add engagement into prerecorded video content.

In some circumstances schools will choose to purchase a pre-made curriculum with included content and videos. Many commercial options are available that provide standards-based online curriculum. These packages are typically designed for fully online learning programs. This takes the burden of content creation off of the shoulders of teachers. It allows them to solely focus on feedback and supporting students' needs. Using pre-made curriculum does have the downside of potentially being a layer of disconnect between teachers and students. It can also cause some curricular misalignment. When teachers create video lessons themselves, it helps maintain the student-teacher relationship. Hearing their own teacher on a video makes the content more personal. It also ensures that the vocabulary and examples are consistent with the curriculum that the school has in place.

It's important for teachers to find balance between which content they create on their own, and when it might be appropriate to use existing content created by other teachers. The endless video library that is YouTube provides teachers supplemental resources that are ready to go. Many education-based Facebook and Twitter communities are full of teachers willing to share their creations.

Many creation platforms, including Seesaw and Flipgrid, have embedded, searchable activity repositories where teachers around the world submit activities to share. Teachers can search by grade, topic, or learning target. It is very important that teachers examine these resources with a critical lens. Does it match my learning targets? Is it an appropriate level of rigor? Will it improve engagement?

Online interactive games, tools, manipulatives, and simulations can also be an important part of asynchronous learning time. These allow students to explore and engage. An example of this might be online math manipulatives to practice a concept like area or fractions. Science teachers might use online simulations such as virtual dissections to explore anatomy or interactive chemical reaction simulators. This can be a way to have some lab-based activities, even in the online learning environment.

Additionally, there are many personalized and adaptive online programs that offer students opportunities to engage with content. Some of these are commercially offered and purchased by schools. There are many platforms that offer similar services free to teachers. These platforms often offer self-paced content with built-in scaffolds to support. If the student answers questions correctly, the learning progresses and new or more challenging content is offered. When students struggle on a topic or standard, the adaptive programs can offer additional practice and video reteaching and scaffolds. When students receive immediate feedback through these digital platforms, students can continue to engage in instruction and practice that is meaningful and relevant to their individual learning progress. On these platforms, teachers can often view activity and data reports to check in on student growth and achievement.

While students are engaging asynchronously, teachers can use the time to evaluate data and offer individual feedback. This feedback may come in the form of written comments left in the learning platforms. Some learning platforms also have features that allow teachers to record audio feedback or make video feedback. While this reinforces the teacher-student relationship and is helpful for learners of all ages, it is especially true for early learners or struggling learners. These students may not yet have adequate literacy skills to review written feedback. Audio and video feedback supports engagement and accessibility for all learners. This can also be a time teachers can meet with small groups or individual students to help support learners with specific learning needs identified during the data evaluation and feedback process.

Creating, Maintaining, and Celebrating the Learning Community

Whatever environment you have to engage with your learners, and whether you engage synchronously or asynchronously, students will often be most engaged when they feel connected to a learning community. Building community is one way we can engage learners who may be hesitant to participate in online learning.

Working in an asynchronous learning environment can sometimes feel lonely and isolating. It's important to provide students opportunities to engage with their peers. This might come in the form of a discussion using the Google Classroom question tool or a discussion forum within an LMS. The learning community can also be fostered through opportunities to see and leave feedback on each other's work. During the 2020 pandemic, some schools used Flipgrid as a way to have school spirit days to bring students together. In place of the traditional Friday theme or dress-up days, the principal would post a Flipgrid topic for all students in the school. Students from many classrooms could record a video for that week's topic and engage with the community by watching videos created by the other students.

Publishing student work to a shared space can help foster that community in the online classroom. It lets students know that the work they do is valued and meaningful. When students feel their work is valued, they will be more likely to continue to engage. Website-based digital portfolios can be used to curate digital content. Portfolios created in Seesaw can also be saved and shared with peers and parents. Both of these examples provide learners with an authentic audience to shine for.

6

Open Education Resources

Anthony Gabriele and Lynn Kleinmeyer

Emergency learning in the pandemic brought to light a number of concerns for school districts, especially the concern of how to transition to a distance learning environment with a lack of resources and/or curricular materials that supported this transition or honored students. However, this exact concern, coupled with our society's unrest and need to examine systemic practices that perpetuate inequities for a large population of students, presents an opportunity for districts and educators to reimagine the delivery of curriculum and instruction, an opportunity in which openly licensed educational resources (referred to in the remainder of the chapter as OER) could be invaluable.

These endeavors are highly important, are real, and are changing the way in which we do business. The focus of this chapter is to provide shared language, common understandings, and tools and ways to do this work.

What Is OER?

Brief History

In 2001, the Massachusetts Institute of Technology's (MIT) faculty proposed to offer, freely and openly, all of their content online, which began the MIT OpenCourseWare project. A short time later, in 2002, the term open education resources (OER) was first coined at the United Nations Educational, Scientific, and Cultural Organization's (UNESCO) Forum on the Impact of Open Courseware for Higher Education in Developing Countries. While this movement originated from developments in open and distance learning in the late 1990s, MIT was credited with "sparking" the OER movement, and the practice of offering free and open resources soon spread. From roughly 2005–2012, numerous studies, reports, and publications were coming out encouraging publishers and governments to make publicly funded education materials available, via the internet, at no cost (https://ocw.mit.edu/about/press-releases/mit-opencourseware-celebrates-15-years-of-open-sharing/; https://drive.google.com/file/d/1OOg6rp289dHCnzwWkOG9tGYKkiGVrSof/view?usp=sharing).

While these initial movements were focused on higher education, OER truly entered the PreK-12 arena in the fall of 2015 as part of former President Obama's 2013 ConnectED initiative. The goal of this initiative was "to enrich K-12 education for every student in America" (https://tech.ed.gov/connected/). According to the US Department of Ed Tech's site (https://tech.ed.gov/connected/), the three core tenets of this initiative were:

1. To connect 99% of students across the country to broadband in five years
2. Empower teachers with the best technology and the training to make the most of it
3. Empower students through individualized learning and rich, digital content

Outcomes and the Larger Context

Two of the more influential initiatives that came out of this work were (1) the #GoOpen Initiative, and (2) the #FutureReady Schools (FRS) Framework (discussed later in the chapter; https://futureready.org/). While the former became the actual catalyst for OER in the PreK-12 arena, the latter is an important movement that has contextualizes and has correlation to the foundational beliefs behind the #GoOpen movement. The US

Department of Education, through the #GoOpen initiative, was committed to supporting

> states, districts and educators using openly licensed educational materials to transform teaching and learning. The #GoOpen initiative and the growing network of States, districts, and educators has not only provided a space for robust discussions about the merits of OER, but also supported broader dialogue and dissemination of information on the policies and practices that impact teaching, learning, and collaboration. #GoOpen State and district leaders are documenting and sharing new approaches to professional learning for teachers, and curating resources that offer students and teachers options for personalizing learning, and strategies to support curating, creating, adapting and sharing OER.
> (https://tech.ed.gov/open/districts/)

> The push to support school districts across the country to adopt OER was also the push to support districts to think differently, think collaboratively, and think equitably. Openly licensed educational resources have enormous potential to increase access to high-quality education opportunities in the United States. Switching to openly licensed educational materials has enabled school districts to repurpose funding typically spent on textbooks for other pressing needs, such as investing in the transition to digital learning.
> (https://tech.ed.gov/open/districts/)

As the OER movement has grown and evolved, so too has how we define OER. As OER entered the K-12 space, a few of the organizations supporting the work have looked to define OER.

- ◆ Teaching, learning, and research resources that reside in the public domain or have been released under a license that permits their free use, reuse, modification, and sharing with others (U.S. Department of Education's National Ed Tech Plan, https://tech.ed.gov/netp/).

- ◆ The myriad of learning resources, teaching practices, and education policies that use the flexibility of OER to provide learners with high quality educational experiences. Creative Commons defines OER as teaching, learning, and research materials that are either (a) in the public domain or (b) licensed in a manner that provides everyone with free and perpetual permission to engage in the 5R activities—retaining, remixing, revising, reusing, and redistributing the resources (William & Flora Hewlett Foundation, https://hewlett.org/strategy/open-education/).

- ◆ Open educational resources (OER) are teaching, learning, and research materials in any medium—digital or otherwise—that reside in the public domain or have been released under an open license that permits no-cost access, use, adaptation, and redistribution by others with no or limited restrictions (UNESCO, https://en.unesco.org/themes/building-knowledge-societies/oer#:~:text=Open%20Educational%20Resources%20(OER)%20are,with%20no%20or%20limited%20restrictions).

- ◆ Open Educational Resources (OER) are teaching, learning, and research materials that are either (a) in the public domain or (b) licensed in a manner that provides everyone with free and perpetual permission to engage in the 5R activities (Creative Commons, https://wiki.creativecommons.org/wiki/What_is_OER%3F).

What OER Is, and What OER Is Not

As outlined in the definitions listed earlier, OER can include a number of different types of learning materials, from lesson plans to singular learning objects to units to complete courses. So you may be wondering how these resources are different from what may already exist in your classroom or school district. In education, there are three types of curricular resources:

- ◆ **Proprietary resources** are those curricular resources that are purchased. These can include textbooks, workbooks, or online learning platforms or tools. These purchases can be a one-time cost or may be paid annually. These resources are often protected by copyright and should be used as the publisher and/or author originally intended.

◆ **Free resources** are those curricular resources that can be found (often online) and used without an associated cost. While these items do not have associated costs, the resources are protected by copyright and should be used as the publisher and/or author originally intended (unless express permission is sought).

◆ **Openly licensed resources** are curricular resources that can be found (often online), used without an associated cost and allow for some modifications, sharing, and/or retention as expressed by the publisher and/or author through a Creative Commons license. These resources can be reused, revised, remixed, retained, and redistributed (these five concepts are known as the 5Rs of OER use; http://opencontent.org/definition/).
(https://help.oercommons.org/support/solutions/articles/42000046846-introduction-to-oer)

During the pandemic, as educators attempted to transition traditional learning materials to a format different from the brick-and-mortar setting, questions of the legalities of copyright and usability began to surface. While educators do have some flexibility to use copyrighted materials for educational purposes under the umbrella of Fair Use, openly licensed resources take the guesswork out of using others' intellectual property. OER make use of Creative Commons licensing, which functions within the boundaries of copyright to allow creators to share some of the usage rights to their intellectual property. The six Creative Commons licenses (https://creativecommons.org/about/cclicenses/) use a combination of license elements to indicate what usage rights are available to end users. Most, but not all, of these license element combinations support the Five Rs of OER (Figure 6.1).

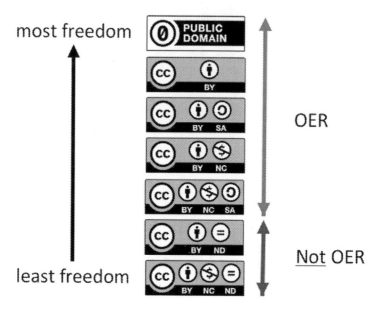

FIGURE 6.1 Infographic of various Creative Commons licenses.
Source: Attributed to Lorna Campbell.

Why OER?

There is often a misconception in education that your curriculum is your textbook or course materials. Curriculum consists of the standards and learning objectives which dictates the content of a course. Rather than allowing the materials to dictate what will be taught, how it will be taught, and when it will be taught (these should be driven by and outlined in the curriculum documents—see the section in this chapter on UbD2.0 and UDL), the materials and resources that are used should be seen and used as a means to support the scope, sequence, and learning outcomes of the curriculum. The resources are but one avenue for supporting "what we use" to help deliver the curriculum. This is a shift in thinking for many educators and provided some challenges for learning during the pandemic. Taking a moment to recognize the constraints of the "materials as curriculum" mentality, allow us to extrapolate the potential that OER has for change in educational practices.

Recognizing Current Constraints (Challenges on Traditional Materials for Both Brick and Mortar and Online)

Many "traditional" curricular resources often function in a very static way and work for a very narrow audience. The constraints of traditional proprietary curricular resources often mean that the materials can only be shared and/or accessed in the ways allowed by the publishers (after purchasing). While many traditional curricular resources have begun to embrace the power of multiple formats, many are still text heavy and perpetuate structures and narratives with limited scope. OER present an opportunity for districts and teachers to move beyond the constraints of traditional formats and narratives to broaden the scope and format of materials to honor the needs and experiences of all students.

As we look to honor our students, an area to consider that has always been and continues, now more than ever, to be incredibly important is providing our students with resources and materials that connect with them, connect them to others, and connect them to the world within which they are living. When thinking about, researching, and selecting materials to support the content, skills, and themes outlined in curriculum, two of the most important questions we can ask are:

- ◆ Do these resources/materials act as both a mirror of and a window to our students lives?
- ◆ Do these resources/materials act as both a mirror of and a window to current society?

We owe it to our students to balance honoring their individual backgrounds with providing them the necessary tools to navigate a diverse, ever-changing world. To this end, the curriculum—learning and transfer goals tied to skills, themes, understandings, and essential questions—should focus not only on skills tied to critical thinking and literacy, but also opportunities to explore ideas around gender, race, sexuality, religion/beliefs, and socioeconomics. When looking to build curriculum for a particular subject area, grade level, and/or course, these questions should drive conversations around a district's beliefs, mission, vision, and long-term transfer goals for that course.

Finding ways to balance the connection between the curriculum (skills and content) we need to teach and our students' lives, interests, and experiences is not always easy. It is essential to consider questions such as:

♦ How do students learn to connect the past to the present?
♦ How do students learn to find common themes throughout what they read that connect to their own lives?
♦ Do students see themselves and their backgrounds and hear their voices represented in what they study?

Taking these questions into consideration and using them as the "lens" by which we address this process is one way to begin to bridge the gap and look to meet our students "where they are."

Embracing the Potential for Change

So how does OER align to other initiatives attempting to shift practice, and what role does OER play in truly shifting practice? While districts across the nation have embraced a number of initiatives aimed at helping to address elements of the Every Student Succeeds Act (ESSA), two paths in particular align themselves with the principles of OER: UbD2.0 and UDL. When leveraged simultaneously, the crosswalk between all three has powerful potential to impact change for students' educational experiences.

Understanding by Design 2.0—a Student-Centered Curriculum Design Framework to Align Student Outcomes to Course Resources

Grant Wiggins and Jay McTighe's Understanding by Design (UbD) framework (https://jaymctighe.com/) has long been one of the staples in the curriculum design world. The latest iteration, Understanding by Design 2.0 (UbD2.0), provides not only a template for structuring curriculum, but a "backwards design" process that ensures alignment from Desired Results (outcomes) to Evidence (assessments) to the Learning Plan (key events and instruction) to Resources (materials) (https://jaymctighe.com/resources/). As we mentioned earlier, delineating the differences between curriculum and the resources we use is essential to this process.

Why is this essential, you may ask?

Many traditional proprietary curricular resources, while claiming to be aligned with Common Core standards, do not align with the more localized learning outcomes or objectives. Using OER allows for the curation and creation of curricular resources/materials that can be contextualized and aligned with local needs. Consider our two options:

- ◆ Traditional approach—Build a curriculum that contains the content, skill, and thematic learning outcomes that align to your state, district, and community expectations, then choose a "textbook" that may or may not align with what you planned.
- ◆ Innovative approach—Build a curriculum that contains the content, skill, and thematic learning outcomes that align to your state, district, and community expectations, then select a variety of high-quality, diverse OER that align to each of your outcomes.

The Garnet Valley School District (GVSD) in Glen Mills, Pennsylvania, which is both a #GoOpen district and a #FutureReady district, continues to be on the forefront of this movement and provides an exemplar of this work in action. The initial district leadership team, from Superintendent Marc Bertrando, to Sam Mormando, the Director of Technology, Innovation, and Online Learning, to Julie Devine, the Supervisor of Digital and Online Learning, to Christine Gumpert, the District Instructional Technology Specialist, and to Dave Pimentel, a Garnet Valley High School social studies teacher, worked collaboratively to begin the process of transitioning to OER, as well as to building an environment that offered students and staff control over "time, path, pace, and place of their learning" (www.garnetvalleyschools. com/home).

The intersection of two major needs—the need to bring back students from cyber charter schools/stop students from leaving for cyber charter schools, along with the need to move to OER—helped Garnet Valley focus on ROI (return on investment and return on instruction), as well as build a systemswide curriculum and course development process in which teachers were trained and compensated to build curriculum and courses that could be offered to support a brick-and-mortar environment, a blended environment, and a fully online environment (which was the district's in-house cyber school, eSchool@GarnetValley).

The Garnet Valley School District Course Development Process includes four stages: student-centered instructional design, student-centered curriculum design, student-centered resource design, and student-centered course design (https://sites. google.com/garnetvalley.org/gvsd-course-development-hub/ home?authuser=0). The first curriculum to go through this process was the Garnet Valley High School's Grade 9 Non-Western Cultures course. The curriculum was written using the UbD2.0 framework, and the two teachers, Christine Gumpert and Dave Pimentel, working in collaboration with the design team from Spider Learning, Inc. (www.spiderlearning.com/), developed the OER Module Flowchart.

As mentioned earlier in this chapter, starting with intentionality was the key to this process. We first worked with the teachers to clearly and deliberately define the student learning outcomes. In the Grade 9 Non-Western Cultures Unit 4, Module 9 Flowchart, the teachers:

+ Developed "Students will be able to" (SWBAT) statements that took the content listed in the Acquisition Skills section of Stage 1: Desired Results of UbD2.0 (see Figure 6.2) and organized them by skill outcome for the students (see Figure 6.3).

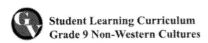
Student Learning Curriculum
Grade 9 Non-Western Cultures

Unit 4 Title: East Asia

Duration of Unit: 3-4 weeks

Anchor Assessment Window: TBD

Unit Summary: The East Asia Unit begins with a survey of the key political and physical locations of the region. Students will be expected to label maps and apply the Five Themes of Geography to this area of the world. The unit then turns attention to the people of the East Asia and their culture. Special focus is given to the Schools of Thought and Buddhism. The political history of China during the dynastic era is covered, and the role of imperialism in the decline of dynastic rule is studied. The birth of the CCP and the superhuman status of Mao Zedong is used as the framework of 20th Century China. Modern day issues in China are addressed, as is China's role as a major regional and world power. Mini-units on Korea and Japan are used to show the similarities and differences of East Asian nations, and to emphasize the role of these nations in the modern world.

	Stage 1 Desired Results	
	Transfer	
Focus Standards/Est Goals for Unit: Established Goals Document	*Students will be able to independently use their learning to...* • Navigate, through the use of maps, in real-world scenarios • Relate to and interact with people from various cultures and faiths. • Analyze current events around the world within historical context.	
Full Complement of PA Standards • Academic Standards for History	*Meaning*	
• Academic Standards for Civics and Government • Academic Standards Economics • Academic Standards for Geography • PA Core - Reading for History and Social Studies • PA Core - Writing for History and Social Studies	OVERARCHING UNDERSTANDINGS *Students will understand that...* • people impact the land and the land impacts people. • people, places, and regions are all interconnected. • societies change over time.	OVERARCHING ESSENTIAL QUESTIONS • How does geography affect the way people live? • How is our world interconnected? • What is the impetus to societal change? • What impacts a person's view of their world?

Understanding by Design 2.0 © 2011 Jay McTighe and Grant Wiggins   Last Updated: January 2018

FIGURE 6.2 Screenshot of GVSD UbD2.0 curriculum document.

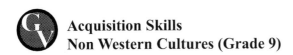
Acquisition Skills
Non Western Cultures (Grade 9)

Current Events and Issues
9. Chinese Regional Hegemony
    One country - two systems (Hong Kong, Macau, Taiwan); Possible secession (Tibet, Xinjiang)
    China's relationship with its neighbors (ASEAN, North Korea, island building, pollution)
    • SWBAT analyze the increasing role of China as a regional and world power.
10. Chinese Domestic Issues
    Population growth and rapid economic growth have made East Asia a leading consumer of natural resources, with far-reaching consequences.
    The Chinese Communist Party is facing increasing pressure (e.g. Tiananmen Square Massacre, Umbrella Revolution, Factory strikes, etc.) from its citizens with regards to pollution, food safety, censorship, corruption, family planning, housing, and civil liberties.

Acquisition
Students will know & be able to... Acquisition Document

FIGURE 6.3 Screenshot of GVSD UbD2.0 curriculum document.

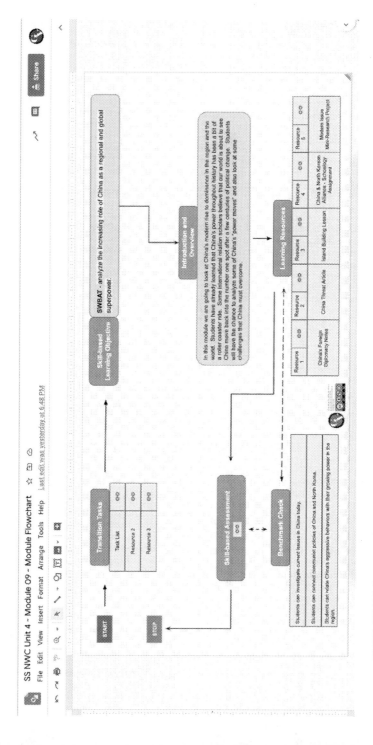

FIGURE 6.4 GVSD UbD2.0 curriculum document.

Current Events and Issues

9. Chinese Regional Hegemony

   One country—two systems (Hong Kong, Macau, Taiwan); possible secession (Tibet, Xinjiang)
   China's relationship with its neighbors (ASEAN, North Korea, island building, pollution)
   ◆ SWBAT analyze the increasing role of China as a regional and world power.
   ◆ Connected the SWBAT to an OER Module Flowchart (see Figure 6.4).
   ◆ Developed five OER-based learning activities/resources that allow students multiple paths to achieve the SWBAT learning outcome (see Figure 6.5).

Learning Resource # 3

Island Building . . . A Modern Approach to Empire Building

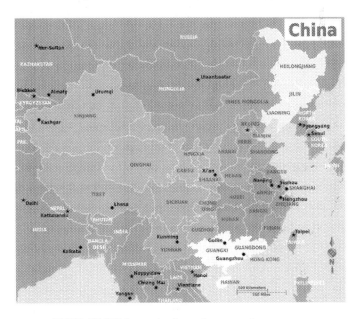

FIGURE 6.5 GVSD UbD2.0 curriculum document.

Source: https://commons.wikimedia.org/wiki/File:Map_of_China_(en).png.

Step 1: Answer this review question

◆ Connection Question . . . During the Age of Imperialism, how did European powers increase the size of their empires?

With almost 1.4 billion people, portions of China are very densely populated. China's government has to be vigilant to ensure that its large population has adequate access to resources. Also, as China modernizes, the economy needs constant fuel and raw materials.

As the map above shows, China is surrounded by either water or other sovereign nations. Unless China wants to start a war by annexing another country's territory, their only option is to push out into the water.

Step 2: Read this article and answer the questions

◆ What is the purpose of a "freedom of navigation" operation?

◆ Why are these mainly uninhabited islands desirable?

When we initially debriefed this process with the teachers, the discussion was around the fact that this really shifted the focus of the curriculum development from "what the teacher wanted to do with the materials" to "what they needed the students to do with the materials." This also ensured a direct connection between the curricular based student outcomes (aligned to standards, content, skills), lessons/activities, and the OER that supported those outcomes.

For more information on the Garnet Valley School District Course Development and Course Digitization processes, as well as samples of the OER curricula, please visit the GVSD Course Development Hub: https://sites.google.com/garnetvalley.org/gvsd-course-development-hub/home.

UDL—Personalizing the Learning Experience by Recognizing and Honoring Learner Needs, Learner Backgrounds, and Experience

Districts across the country are beginning to recognize that traditional instructional design and materials work for a small sector of their student population. These districts recognize that personalizing student learning is an essential practice to reach those for whom traditional methods and materials are not working. To this end, many districts are exploring the principles of Universal Design for Learning (UDL).

Created by the Center for Applied Special Technologies (CAST) (www.cast.org/about#.XvOlcZNKhTY), the UDL framework guides educators in the intentional design of learning opportunities that reduce barriers and and honor learners throughout the learning process, making learning environments and experiences more inclusive and engaging. The updated UDL Guidelines (http://udlguidelines.cast.org/), released in 2018, encourage educators to provide students with multiple means of "Engagement" (how students connect to and plan for the learning experience), "Representation" (how students interact with content), and "Action & Expression" (how students demonstrate their understanding of the content). Figure 6.6 gives an overview of the Universal Design for Learning Guidelines.

Throughout the entirety of the UDL Guidelines, educators are called to provide students with choice and voice, planning for multiple ways for students to engage with content. As noted previously, oftentimes traditional curricular materials are static, especially in regards to format and accessibility.

As with any good instructional design, the exploration of OER must start with an understanding of your learners. Keeping in mind this lens of knowing and honoring learners allows for a direct correlation between the use of OER and the principles of UDL in moving towards personalization. For districts looking to maximize the powerful potential of personalization, OER offer a solution devoid of major financial investment and leave space to ensure that students see themselves represented in instructional materials.

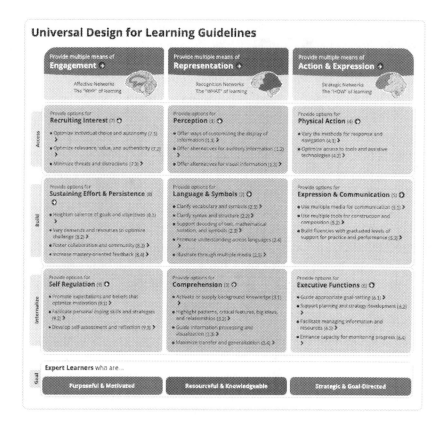

FIGURE 6.6 Screenshot of UDL Framework.

Source: Taken from http://udlguidelines.cast.org/.

Where and How Do I Find Resources?

Now that you have the background and the connections, you are probably wondering where to start the exploration process. Ideally, a team of educators would work through the procurement process. However, we also recognize that there are a number of innovative educators who may want to explore OER as instructional resources for their students. Regardless of the team or individual approach, we recommend exploration with intentionality. To this end, we recommend the following process.

Begin With the Priorities: Students and Standards

As with any acquisition of curricular materials and/or resources, the journey begins with the prioritization of students and standards. As educators, it is extremely important that you know your learners, their learning styles, preferences, and needs, but also their backgrounds and experiences. These factors play an integral role in students' educational experiences and should play an integral role in the selection and use of curricular resources. There are any number of approaches to getting to know your students, including a variety of learner profiles (just googling the term provides any number of examples and templates), but we encourage you to consider questions that also delve into learner identity, asking for students to explore how they identify themselves, as well as additional factors like home environment. Coupled with one-on-one interactions, these inventories and profiles can be powerful tools to be used in designing educational experiences that are equitable and inclusive.

Simultaneously, it's essential that educators have a deep grasp of the standards and learning targets/objectives. As referenced in the earlier section on UbD, keeping student learning outcomes in mind while examining instructional materials to ensure alignment between the resource and the objective is equally as important.

Conduct a Needs Assessment

Once the students being served and the standards being addressed are firmly in mind, the next step is to do a needs assessment. It is important to take stock of the curricular resources already available, but we suggest considering the following:

- ◆ Which of your curricular resources are working to address the standards?
- ◆ In which settings do your curricular resources function well (i.e., face-to-face in a classroom environment, in an online environment)?

♦ Which of your students stand to benefit the most from these resources? Which of your students stand to benefit the least?

♦ Do your curricular resources support a variety of formats, including reflections of learner preferences and accessibility features to support learner interaction?

The answers to these questions can help narrow the focus for exploration as educators progress through the next steps.

Determine Quality Criterion

Based on the needs of your students, the standards to be addressed, your instructional beliefs and the results of your needs assessment, it is important to determine what curricular resources you will consider using. Just as with a traditional adoption model, we encourage districts and educators to determine their quality criterion for consideration (beyond standards alignment). For example, ask yourself the following:

♦ Is it essential that the resources be available in or easily translatable to multiple languages?

♦ Is it essential that the materials have built-in accessibility features or work well with third-party accessibility tools?

♦ Is it essential that materials be usable both online and offline?

The good news is that a number of organizations have already done the work of creating resources to vet OER. Both the Achieve (www.achieve.org/publications/achieve-oer-rubrics) and the Educators Evaluating the Quality of Instructional Products (EQuIP) (www.achieve.org/our-initiatives/equip/all-equip-resources/rubrics-and-feedback-forms) rubrics provide robust examinations of OER, ranging from evaluations of standards alignment to the quality of explanation of subject matter.

Many districts have taken these rubrics and adapted them to reflect additional quality criterion in alignment with district beliefs. For example, Grossmont Union High School in California created a modified version of the above rubrics to reflect their district values for curriculum materials adoption (https://docs.google.com/document/d/1qACdG2Tuo4kHLQEwVzppjomp0qSyFNQ5ZwnfaWpTA0I/edit?usp=sharing). Cedar Rapids School District in Iowa created their own revised OER rubric to integrate questions about accessibility features of OER to support vulnerable students.

With your students, standards, and quality criterion in mind, it is now time to begin your exploration of OER!

Curate (and Create) Resources

As the #GoOpen movement has gained traction in PreK-12 districts across the nation, repositories housing OER have grown exponentially. These repositories have a variety of resources, ranging from "turn-key" curricular materials (those that are packaged in a ready-to-use way) to individual learning items. Some repositories are specific in focus, while others share numerous resources spanning a number of grade levels and subjects.

For those unfamiliar with OER, we would recommend starting with the "Resources for Getting Started" list of repositories compiled by New America (www.newamerica.org/education-policy/reports/making-connections-prek12-oer-in-practice/resources-to-get-started/). This annotated list provides not only links to various repositories, but also provides some context as to grade levels, subject matter, and/or any additional notes of importance, making it invaluable as a beginning place for exploration. The additional benefit of this curated list is that it provides representation from a whole gamut of OER contributors, from nonprofit organizations to states to individual districts.

While the resources being contributed to OER repositories are growing exponentially by the day, there may also be a need to create some resources to meet your needs. This creation and contribution by educators around the nation is a vital part of the OER community and is the underpinning of the whole movement.

Share the Resources

Whether you are curating "turn-key," remixing and revising, or creating your own content, the final step is to share the materials with your students (and colleagues, if applicable). Most OER is teacher-facing. As part of the process, you will need to determine what resources will actually be shared with students and in what way. Your sharing considerations must take into account how your students will be interacting with the materials. Some OER are naturally going to be shared online in a digital format (such as simulations and videos), while others can be downloaded and printed for students. If your district and students have access to technology and have been using a learning management system, we encourage you to consider using those tools to continue to share curricular materials with your students. However, during the pandemic, families and districts across the nation felt the ramifications of the digital divide. You must take into account the realities of access for your students outside of your brick-and-mortar setting. If there is a barrier to digital access, determine what resources will be downloaded and printed and create a distribution plan.

Putting OER in Context (and Bringing It All Together)

While OER work has been happening in a number of districts across the country for roughly the past five years, the choice to do so was exactly that, a *choice*. Whether that choice was driven by an internal drive for growth and evolution, or by external pressures to address matters of instruction, curriculum, assessment, resources, equity, inclusivity, or fiscal responsibility, the current state of the world, and therefore education, is demanding that educators think differently, think creatively, and adapt accordingly.

However, educators across the nation recognize that the time for change is now. At some level, educators do not have a "choice" anymore. Our current societal climate demands the need for a system that honors our individual and collective backgrounds, perspectives, and voices. At the same time, states across the nation are discussing ways to safely and effectively reopen in the fall. While it has already had a place in *some* states and districts, the "new norm" for *all* of us looks to be offering our students and families a variety of options for school, spanning the gamut from traditional brick-and-mortar with some modifications to fully online and virtual, to some combination, hybrid, or blend in between.

The use of OER to support curriculum and address equity and inclusion, no matter the educational setting, can provide districts with a viable option to address both as we move forward and reimagine education.

Resources to Learn More

We fully recognize that this chapter was just the beginning of a conversation. While we hope we left you with a deeper understanding of what OER are, how they can serve you and your students, and how to begin your journey, we want to provide you with additional resources to continue building your capacity and join the OER conversation, as well as delve deeper into some concepts briefly reference in the chapter.

To learn more about OER, we encourage you to explore:

- CCSSO OER One-Pager: https://docs.google.com/ document/d/1pdZihtzIrYXrPHonMgJmcV32oa3_ yW0SCqlFVHR5uGc/edit?ts=5a8dda56
- Education Week Open Educational Resources: Overview and Definition: www.edweek.org/ew/issues/open-educational-resources-oer/index.html
- New America "Revise, Remix, Redesign" OER Podcast: www.newamerica.org/education-policy/podcasts/ revise-remix-redesign/
- New America Prek-12 OER in Practice: www.newamerica. org/education-policy/reports/making-connections-prek12-oer-in-practice/
- New America YouTube Playlist: www.youtube.com/play list?list=PLNoVefpaPtVMH0v2sOONT3uPArh47sq8r
- US Department of Education Office of Ed Tech: https:// tech.ed.gov/open/districts/
- OER Commons Introduction to OER: https://help. oercommons.org/support/solutions/articles/42000046846-introduction-to-oer

To learn more about other ideas referenced in the chapter, we encourage you to explore:

- Creative Commons Licensing: https://creativecommons.org/licenses/
- #FutureReady Schools (FRS) Framework: https://futureready.org/
- The National Center for Accessible Educational Materials: http://aem.cast.org/
- Understanding by Design 2.0 (UbD2.0): https://jaymctighe.com/
- Universal Design for Learning (UDL): http://udlguidelines.cast.org/

7

Flipping the Online Classroom

Stephanie Filardo

Introduction: What, Why, and a Call to Action

What Is Flipped Instruction?

Flipped instruction is the practice of swapping what are traditionally "in class" activities and "homework" activities. In flipped instruction, students take part in the learning activity (reading, video, research, etc.) prior to class and use class time for other learning activities. For example, in a traditional classroom, I would introduce and deliver a lesson on solving one-step equations in class, then have students complete practice problems as homework. In a flipped model, I might assign an instructional video for my students to watch and have students complete a few problems as homework. The class time is then open for practice and additional higher-level activities.

Many teachers have been utilizing this model in their physical classrooms and it is possible to apply to the online classroom as well. Online instruction lends well to a flipped model because it may not be possible for all students to join a live class session. Teachers who have more than one section of a class/subject will feel these benefits quickly as they realize it isn't necessary to host multiple lectures each day. In utilizing a flipped model of online instruction, we will separate activities by what can be done synchronously (full or small group) and asynchronously (small group/individually).

Why Flipped Instruction?

Particularly as we prepare for a school year in which classes may fluctuate between meeting in person and online, flipped instruction can help educators make the most of face-to-face time with students as well as their own planning time. The purpose of this chapter is to serve as a launching point to those who are looking at changing their teaching to work more efficiently in a digital classroom space. A search for "flipped instruction" will turn up many amazing resources. I encourage you to do more research on this rather than taking my word for it. What you will find in this chapter is perspective and guidance on designing an online flipped learning environment as well as consideration for social-emotional learning (SEL) and digital inequity.

Who Benefits?

Since traditional schooling as we know it began, students have needed to be absent for various reasons. Excuses range from obvious (doctor's appointment, illness, college visit) to frustrating (family vacation, sporting event, unknown). I say that these reasons are frustrating because it places a burden on teachers to ensure students are receiving instruction while they are gone and the reason isn't necessarily seen as important. Regardless of the reason, there are student and teacher absences every day. It is common to hear teachers' lounge conversations around "so-and-so was absent again and didn't ask for work." When teachers flip the classroom, they post their plans and instructions for students in an online space. This allows students who have been absent to access what has been missed. It's just good practice.

Students who benefit from this aren't just those who need to be out sick. I've had multiple students over the years who were backup childcare for younger siblings. This resulted in strings of missed days and difficulty getting and making up work. While opinions differ on whether this is right, these students didn't have a choice. With several aspects of their lives already working to their disadvantage, access to education and learning materials from home didn't need to be one of them.

At the same time, I have had students miss several weeks in the winter due to traveling out of the country to visit family. This may be seen as frivolous travel, but family and vacations are important. If we've learned anything during this pandemic, I hope it is the value we should be placing on family and wellness. Sure, not everyone can do it. Yes, it would be more convenient for us if families arranged travel during scheduled school breaks. No, we don't actually have any control over that. Because I have been flipping my classroom, rather than putting together weeks worth of lessons at a moment's notice, I can instruct my students to check Google Classroom for the assignments when they are able to.

As I write this, my district is rolling out plans for online, blended, or in-person instruction this fall. Many parents have already requested fully online instruction for the 2020–2021 school year. Even if we begin in-person, we can anticipate needing to be online at some points during the year as COVID-19 cases are identified and schools need to be closed for cleaning. As a teacher, I also need to be prepared in the event of my own absence. Teaching while sick is often joked about because "it's easier than making sub plans." This is not something we can allow, both for our health and sanity.

Designing Online Classroom Spaces

For a flipped classroom to be successful, the teacher must transition from a mindset of being the "sage on the stage" to a facilitator of learning experiences. The online structure, often a learning management software (LMS), will include more than a way to deliver instruction; it will also engage the students in the learning process, with opportunities for teacher feedback and peer collaboration. Other important aspects to consider when designing online classrooms are fostering the social and emotional needs of students and problem solving to ensure digital inequity.

Transition From Teacher to Facilitator

Flipped instruction is a mindset shift from a traditional class-room since students will be taking on more of a direct role in learning the information. In a traditional classroom setting or online setting using teaching from live lectures, the teacher is the expert, in control of how, when, and where students learn. Flipped instruction shifts the teacher to the role of facilitator, one who guides students through learning experiences and reflects on their learning with them through additional activities. Some are ready for this shift; others need a bit of guidance. This chapter is intended to serve as a guide for those who are ready as well as those who might need a little more convincing to make the jump.

Since there is another chapter specifically on engagement, both synchronous and asynchronous, I won't go into as much detail here. The main idea is that flipped instruction includes a combination of synchronous and asynchronous learning activities. In traditional instruction, the new knowledge piece is in the classroom as a whole class activity (synchronous setting) and the homework/practice/extension is outside of class (asynchronous setting). In flipped instruction, the settings are switched. Students work through individual learning activities independently and then come together for discussions and other collaborative learning activities. However, there is no rule that says the learning activities have to be individual. Teachers can choose what is best for the lesson and content.

Flipped Instruction Is More Than Just a Video

Flipped instruction is often thought of as video lectures. While this is one way of going about it, there are many ways to practice flipped instruction. I find it best to consider the Universal Design for Learning (UDL)[1] framework. UDL best practice is to offer multiple means of representation for learning new information that does not depend on just one of the senses (sight, hearing, touch, etc.). This means options for activities ranging the spectrum of audio, visual, and text. Students are then given some choice and are able to access the information in the mode that has the least barriers for them. This is different from learning styles, but students' personal preference can also play a part in their choice. For example, students could:

◆ Conduct online research about a topic or one aspect of a topic
◆ Read chapters from a book
◆ Listen to a podcast
◆ Watch a documentary

Teachers also provide resources to help parents/guardians understand the methods/process when leading the instruction with their children.

When beginning to build a flipped classroom and incorporate UDL, my recommendation is to take it slow. While your goal may be to offer multiple means of representation for every lesson, it is perfectly fine to start with one. The nature of why we are looking into online and blended instruction at this time is due to pandemic. This is not the time for you to stress yourself out trying to make everything perfect. Perhaps just make a goal that you will use different modes of learning as you go through lessons, choosing what works best for your students and the content at the time. If that happens to be a YouTube video, then it happens to be a video. There is no prize for spending the most time on this. Compare your journey with online instruction and learning to yourself, not others. Teaching is not a competitive sport. Be inspired. Learn. Grow. Repeat.

I did then what I knew how to do.
Now that I know better, I do better.
Maya Angelou

When beginning my journey of flipping and personalizing my special education math classroom eight years ago, I took on too much by insisting on making my own video for every lesson and burnt out quickly. I spent many of my evenings planning out, recording, and editing videos. The nice thing is those videos still exist for me to direct students to and I can continue adding to them, but it should be more of a long-term goal or even divided amongst a department or team of teachers rather than just one person. If you have students who prefer a live lecture and you want to continue that, you can also record the class for others to access. This wouldn't be my first choice as you aren't using the live class time for other learning activities, but you could offer it as an optional lecture for those who are interested. There are many wonderful resources already available (many will be linked at the end of this chapter) that do not require you to "reinvent the wheel." It is not a goal of flipped instruction or online teaching for you to do everything all by yourself. Utilize credible resources and your personal learning network whenever possible.

Not sure where to start? Post your question to Twitter with these hashtags in your message: #flippedlearning #flippedclass #flipclass #flippedclassroom #edchat #edtech. Be sure to include any hashtags relevant to your content area and learning networks. Hashtags on social media are like search terms. It helps connect you to the relevant audience. People who do not follow you but follow these hashtags will see your post. Figure 7.1 provides a visual outline for what a social media post might look like when seeking resources.

Educators, such as Jonathan Spike, @jonathanspike, are often willing to share their strategies. He shared with me in a reply on Twitter (Figure 7.2) that he likes to use digital breakouts to introduce concepts in flipped instruction. Additionally, Jonathan provided access to an example for me to share with readers of this book. It is linked in the resources at the end of the chapter.

FIGURE 7.1 Example Tweet for #flippedclassroom resources.

Jonathan Spike @jonathanspike · Jun 24
Replying to @i3algebra
Send out clues to a digital breakout to different members of
a group - have them work together on their clues to solve
the overall breakout using new info they research on the
topic.

FIGURE 7.2 Tweet from Jonathan Spike, @JonathanSpike.

By now, you might be thinking, "This is great, but what about the students who don't do the pre-work (independent learning activity) prior to our class meeting?" or "How do I know they have done the pre-work?" This is when we attach some sort of accountability piece to the learning activity. Think of it as what you might normally do for an exit ticket or a bell ringer. You can have students complete a survey providing some insight into their learning. For example, post a question in Google Classroom, or use a Google Form linked through your LMS. Use caution when adding accountability activities such as these—keep them brief. Students are not motivated by busy work. Your time is also better served working with students and curating content. A method I use with my students involves the students completing a learning log (example linked in resources at the end of the chapter). This works well when students are working on different concepts (either by grouping/design or through independent learning tracks). Students use this as a way to communicate their progress and also briefly journal their thoughts on the learning activities. I then have reflection questions for each week. This type of setup allows for students to use a single document for accountability and communication.

I'm not promising this will be some magical fix-all. There are still students who will have trouble engaging with online instruction. Some students do better with more guidance. You can win this battle in the feedback portion and by cutting down on overly repetitive practice or drills. In my previous (high school special education) and current (middle school gifted) math classrooms, flipped learning led to personalized paths for learning. I enjoyed becoming a guide or facilitator to the content as opposed to what previously felt like a broken record of direct instruction multiple times a day. If you've ever questioned "Did I already say this?" during a lesson with your class, you can rest assured flipped teaching will not leave you wondering. I recall often feeling bad for my first class because my explanation got better as the day went on! Flipped instruction allows you to purposefully curate the content students need to learn and explore.

For me, the benefits of flipped instruction outweigh the drawbacks. Students are able to take the time they need with learning materials and use time with peers and their teacher to extend this knowledge. Even with the new content portion of class occurring asynchronously, the involvement of the teacher is vital in this process.

Classroom Management in the Online Classroom

When creating a successful online classroom, it is important to take into account the overall classroom management you will use. Just as with the physical space, students crave and need organization, assistance and support for executive function skills (and deficits), routines, predictability, and open lines of communication with teachers and peers. Because organization varies widely across contents and grade levels, I am including some questions for you to consider:

Organization
◆ What platform/LMS are other teachers in your school/district using? (Aim for consistency.)
◆ What platform will you use?
◆ Will you organize by date, topic, or unit?
◆ Will students be able to access all content, or will you post as you go?
◆ How will you teach this organization to students and parents?

Executive Function Skills
◆ In what ways will your system support students with their organization?
  ◆ Assignments on digital calendar
  ◆ Email reminders when assignments are posted
◆ In what ways will your system support students with their focus?

♦ Are you working with students to help identify efficient working practices? Times of day when they are most focused? Encouraging mindfulness and breaks?

Routines/Predictability

♦ Will you have office hours?
♦ Will you have regular class meetings?
♦ What can students expect from you?
♦ What do you expect from students?
♦ Norms for video calls
♦ Norms for emails
♦ Where are your FAQs?

Communication

♦ How are you communicating all of the above?
♦ In what ways are you reaching out to students?
♦ In what ways are you reaching out to parents?
♦ How and when are you available to students and parents?
♦ In what ways can students communicate with each other?
♦ In what ways are other teachers in your school/district communicating?

With all of the above questions, aim for consistency, when possible.

As part of the process of becoming an ISTE Certified Teacher, I learned a great deal about what makes a good online learning environment. I recommend additionally using the ISTE Standards for Teachers as a guide in this process. The link is included with the resources at the end of this chapter.

Maintaining Teacher Presence in the Learning Process

Even the best technology tools cannot replace a teacher. Flipped instruction is *not* posting all of your lecture slides assignments for the year and just sitting back while students do the work. Flipped instruction is not easier, yet it isn't harder either. It's different. The teacher still plays a very important role. For many of the reasons mentioned in the classroom management section, students need facilitation as part of their learning. Even the most self-driven students need feedback and guidance.

In the classroom, my presence was known because I walked around the room as students worked. I would ask questions and provide feedback as I noticed what students were working on and what learning conversations they were having. My students have told me on many occasions over the years that I answer questions with questions. To me, this is one of the greatest compliments of my teaching. Answering a student question does not help learning if they can be guided to find the answer. Part of this classroom management and learning practice comes from something I learned in a psychology course in college: the concept that you can change something just by observing it. Would my students have been learning with me sitting at my desk? Probably. Was their learning better because I was watching it closely? I think so. I also believe students saw and understood my expectations because of my interaction. (For the record, I haven't had a teacher desk for over five years.) The same applied to supervising students while working online; my observation just looked a little different.

The capabilities for student-teacher interaction will vary by grade level, district, and technology access, but you will need to find a way to gather your students for synchronous learning activities. You should have a schedule that includes small group or class meetings and flipped days (a day without a class meeting with a pre-work/learning assignment). Other days to consider would be project days, in which students would be meeting with smaller groups with or without your supervision. This could also be a great way to include time for working on personalized learning projects or passion projects. There are many possibilities, but this may look like:

- ◆ Daily class meetings (pre-work done each night)
- ◆ Monday/Wednesday class meetings, Tuesday/Thursday flipped days
- ◆ Monday/Wednesday flipped days, Tuesday/Thursday class meetings, Friday project days

What you do during these class meetings depends greatly on the content. The advice I give when training teachers to use video conferencing is:

> *Don't leave your students thinking "This should have been an email."*

When we gather people together, it should be to connect. If it's just to disseminate information, consider making a video. Breakout rooms can be used in Zoom (and soon Google Meet) for teachers to facilitate small group activities virtually. Paired with shared documents or other online collaborative tools, video conferencing becomes more powerful. It can be used for brainstorming, debate, Socratic seminar, presentations, etc.

There are many authors and scientists who have made themselves available to join virtual classes as guest speakers. One of my favorite resources, Skype a Scientist, arranged guest speakers through their YouTube channel each week, but I didn't gather students to watch this live in a video chat. I shared the link and let them watch on their own. If they missed it live, they could watch the archived video on the channel. An appropriate assignment for this might be for students to ask two questions (even if not asking live) and share two things they learned. The class could then share this information and have further discussion during the next class meeting. Again, you are facilitating. It doesn't always have to mean you're doing all the heavy lifting.

In addition to class meetings, office hours are a great way for students to seek out assistance. Starting in March 2020, I scheduled a block of time each day where I was available in our class Google Meet. I asked students, in addition to completing the learning log (mentioned earlier), to check in during office hours at least once per week. This was a great time for students to ask questions, get help on concepts, or just have some social interaction. Not all students checked in. That was okay. For students who did not check in, I spent part of office hours time checking their learning log and making comments or sending an email. For some students, I would send the link to a game or a link to a video for something they were interested in. Often, when students didn't check in, it was their way of saying, "I'm good." In addition to assistance, office hours can also be a fun interaction. I switched Wednesdays to Game Day and it was, by far, the most attended office hour of the week. This was a great opportunity for us to have fun together and we all came to look forward to these days. My students even requested to schedule game days over the summer as well as a way to stay connected.

Teacher Feedback (Accountability vs Grades)

Since schools began closing in March 2020, I have been part of more conversations about grading than I can count. Prior to schools transitioning to distance instruction, I had also been involved in many conversations about grading. While I am bound by building and district grading policies, I find myself grading less and less as the years go on.

The purpose of school is for students to learn. What do we do when students don't do the activities? I don't throw my hands up into the air and say "better luck next time." It's my job to help the students learn. It's also my job to understand why they haven't done the assignment. If a student does not turn in an assignment, it doesn't mean they don't know the content. The absence of data does not imply no learning occurred, it means they didn't turn in the assignment. For me, assessments (in many forms) give a better picture of what students know than things done as homework or practice. Math lends well to mastery-based learning. I tend to believe all subjects do. While the purpose of this chapter isn't to convince you to adapt this policy, I feel this is important to mention because grades do not equal accountability.

I ask students to bring their problems to class. We work through math problems to ensure understanding. This may not seem like much, but when students are expected to come with their math homework completed, it doesn't exactly set the expectation that not everyone is going to understand the assignment. This way, students have attempted a few problems, more if they wished, and aren't expected to be proficient yet. They are primed for more learning as opposed to being beaten down or made to feel shame over needing help. In my class, practice is mastery-based. The expectation is for students to master the practice. They get feedback, not a grade. Again, I have used this with students who have a wide range of math abilities and learning needs. It actually worked better with those who were at-risk. I wouldn't do it any other way.

Meaningful feedback is something that drives learning forward. Any work can be improved upon. If you are asking students to produce work, you should provide feedback. If you aren't prepared to do that, then consider not assigning the work.

Peer Collaboration

We are fortunate to live in a time where technology can help us connect when we cannot be together. Just as this works for class, this also works for students. There is an opportunity for students to work with peers using the same technology we connect as a class. Chances are that great project or activity you were going to have students work on in person can be adapted to work for a virtual connection. This also provides constructive opportunities for students to communicate with their peers and continue working on project management skills.

Questions to Consider:

♦ What opportunities will I provide for students to comment on each others' work?
♦ What opportunities will I provide for students to work with their peers?

Problem Solving for Equity

No chapter on flipped instruction would be complete without mentioning that devices and internet access are required to fully access the learning opportunities. Much of this chapter was written with the assumption that students have technology access. The reality is that not all students will have access and not all homes will have enough access after all persons in the household are taken into account. Many public libraries have devices and wifi hotspots to check out. Schools are sometimes able to pair with libraries to write grants to help provide this access. Unfortunately, I don't have a solution to the greater issue, but I am actively advocating for progress and change. In the meantime, this will mean adapting activities so that all students are able to participate.

Questions to Consider for Students (and Yourself):

♦ Do students have internet access at home?
♦ Is the bandwidth sufficient for everyone who needs to access?
♦ Do students have devices at home?
♦ Even if using school-provided devices, will students be sharing this device with others in their home?
♦ Will access to devices/internet limit ability to participate in synchronous class activities?
♦ Will parents need to be home to supervise student learning?
♦ Will parents need to be available to teach content to students?
♦ How will you support parents and/or work with them to teach your students?

Inspiration and Resources

It is my hope this chapter has served to illuminate some of the possibilities regarding transitioning to a flipped instruction model. The best advice I can offer is, start small, connect with others to share (reliable, quality) resources, and don't stress about grading everything. Most importantly, focus on experiences for your synchronous time together. Your students will thank you. I strongly believe you will appreciate it as well. Again, this is not meant to be the only resource you access. It is a starting point. What follows are some of my favorite resources for curating content as well as some inspiration.

Happy flipping!

Ms. Filardo's E-Learning Log: https://bit.ly/FilardoELearning

ISTE Standards for Educators: www.iste.org/standards/for-educators

Jonathan Spike's Digital Breakout Resource Folder: https://bit.ly/SpikeBreakout or
https://drive.google.com/drive/folders/1wUz7aKD1RMfOR-QNWW74dO9rI4C2SFmT

Virtual Nerd (6–8 Math, Algebra, Geometry, Algebra 2): http://virtualnerd.com/

Crash Course (ELA, Social Studies, Digital Citizenship, Engineering, Science): www.youtube.com/user/crashcourse

Crash Course Kids (Space Science, Engineering, Physical Science, Earth Science): www.youtube.com/user/crashcoursekids

PBS Idea Channel (good conversation/debate topics): www.youtube.com/channel/UC3LqW4ijMoENQ2Wv17ZrFJA

PBS Voices (Documentary Channel): www.youtube.com/channel/UCq6OAftTQOuUBRdtUDq5SUA

PBS Eons: www.youtube.com/channel/UCzR-rom72PHN9Zg7RML9EbA

Physics Girl: www.youtube.com/user/physicswoman

Gross Science: www.youtube.com/user/grossscienceshow/videos

Numberphile: www.youtube.com/channel/UCoxcjq-8xIDTYp3uz647V5A

Netflix Documentaries (access without a Netflix account or subscription): www.youtube.com/playlist?list=PLvahqwMqN4M0GRkZY8WkLZMb6Z-W7qbLA

John Spencer: www.youtube.com/user/OurSocialVoice

I recommend checking out John's collection of video writing prompts and the video "There's No Single Right Way to Do Distance Learning": https://youtu.be/OykqwbxlPmg

CultofPedagogy—8GreatEducationalPodcastsforKids:www.cultofpedagogy.com/educational-podcasts-for-kids/

Common Sense Education—Flipped Example ELA: www.commonsense.org/education/articles/teaching-shakespeare-in-a-flipped-classroom

Common Sense Education—Flipped Example Math: www.commonsense.org/education/articles/peek-inside-a-flipped-math-classroom

Note

1. Universal Design for Learning: http://udlguidelines.cast.org/representation.

8

Teaching for Equity, Inclusion, and Representation Online

Yaritza Villalba

In a perfect world, all students would have access to technology, instructional resources, and most importantly, the ability to engage in curricula and standards that are culturally relevant. Culturally responsive teaching or culturally relevant teaching is grounded on the educator showing knowledge in teaching in a multicultural setting. It is a cultural component and recognizes the importance of including your students' cultural references in all aspects of learning. This includes knowing where your students come from, acknowledging their diverse preferences of learning, and most importantly using strategies and practices that encourage students to relate what is being taught or introduced to their communities, families, and culture.

The first step to becoming a culturally responsive teacher is communicating high expectations for your students and having a positive perspective on their culture and family relationships. It is important to use student prior knowledge to guide your classroom discussions. What you may notice is that your students' perspective on the content you are introducing will be different from his or her counterparts; this is normal. Activating students' prior knowledge allows you, as the instructor, to further understand how a student's experiences impact their true understanding and opinions surrounding the content.

Another aspect of culturally responsive pedagogy is your classroom culture. What books are you offering your students? In order to equip students with text, they may be interested in reading, considering diverse authors should be your first step. Also, think of the context of the books. Be sure to create and build a diverse inventory of books in your library that include stories and history that reflect urban families and the LGBTQ community. Suggested authors that come to mind when considering culturally responsive teaching and equity are Gholdy Muhammad and Ibram X. Kendi. Both authors explore the importance of identity and anti-racism and give readers a critical analysis of culturally and historically responsive literacy. Classroom culture also includes your communication with students, the posters/images around your classroom, and whether you have created an environment where students feel cared for and appreciated.

When referring to online learning, the images, posters, and videos that you decide to project during a Zoom or Google Meet conference should always reflect the students you are teaching. Teaching online was once the "new norm" for most teachers and as we are transitioning into teaching students face-to-face or in a blended setting, we must keep in mind the skills and adaptive strategies we had to learn in order to effectively teach students. Teaching online has required that teachers reflect on their old/traditional pedagogical methods of teaching and acknowledge the need for new strategies and a better understanding of how students learn. This "new norm" has challenged some of the traditional frameworks for education that have always been proven to be ineffective, i.e., lectures, textbook readings, handouts, and most importantly, standardized testing. All of these are systems that provide one desired outcome. Standardized testing, or artificial parameters of testing, has always proven to be ineffective. Not every student learns the same, yet we continue to structure our lessons, activities, and assessments based on the notion that they do. According to Sir Ken Robinson (2010), we have created an educational system that functions as if it were a production line, which does not enable students to be independent learners and collaborators and thus, they are not prepared to compete for 21st-century jobs. We have designed curricula, online and for in-school sessions, that are not encouraging students to become critical thinkers.

While many school districts thrive best on tradition, distance learning has proven that traditional frameworks for teaching do not encourage all students to take ownership of their learning and use skills like critical thinking, problem solving, and collaboration to make connections with the world around them. With remote learning, many states ruled out the requirement for students to have to pass a standardized test in order to graduate. This pivotal decision allowed teachers to be more creative and intentional when creating opportunities online. We began to notice a shift in teaching. Teachers created more project-based learning (PBL) tasks, as opposed to basic question and answer activities. This proved, all along, teachers and educators have had the tools to engage students in learning.

The reality is that this world is not perfect and "distance learning" or the idea of teaching students through an online platform has revealed the necessity to teach for equity, inclusion, and representation of all students online. This means it is time for you to ditch any assumptions or misconceptions you once had about teaching online and allow yourself to truly meet the needs of each individual student. If you are ready to dive in, let's talk about the difference between equality and equity.

Equity

In the landmark 1954 case *Brown v. Board of Education*, Supreme Court Justice Earl Warren ruled that in the field of public education, the doctrine of "separate but equal," which was constitutionally upheld by the 1896 case of *Plessy v. Ferguson*, was unconstitutional and had no place. What this meant was segregation in education deprived African Americans the right to be provided with an adequate education and the full opportunity to be successful. Although this decision overturned the *Plessy* decision and integrated "public" education, it failed to address the disparities within the system itself that educators are still tackling today.

Children of color are not given the same opportunities as their wealthy white counterparts to successfully compete for careers. Equality was defined by the *Plessy v. Ferguson* decision. Consequently, it proved that this nation understood the effects of inequality and that as long resources were made available (no matter the amount or if it failed to address the unique needs of Black and Brown students) that was equal. Equity is ensuring that students of color, who are often low-income students, have access to a higher quality of education by teachers and administrators who understand the importance of meeting each student where they are.

Many have asked, how do you provide equity through teaching online? Equity is about providing students with resources that would enable them to engage with content in a way that is tailored to their unique individual needs. Equity requires teachers to think beyond the hardware of technological tools and look closely into how the tools benefit or hinder the learning of students. It is understanding each student and preparing their online experience in a fashion that encourages the student to be creative, critical thinkers, and explorers. To fully understand what equity in education is, one must first analyze the disparities that exist in communities and across state lines.

The ultimate goal of education is to create human capital. As any other business, funding sources are dependent on the stakeholders involved and assistance from federal and/or state governments. Sadly, the power to regulate education is reserved to the state government, which widens the achievement gap for low socioeconomic communities. Disparities, or economic differences between regions or countries, are the underlying cause of the increasing gap in the academic achievement of children of color and their white counterparts. States lack the funding to appropriately provide adequate resources to all schools, thus encouraging other stakeholders, like families who pay high property taxes, to fund school districts.

Sadly this has been true, way before remote learning. In low socioeconomic communities, people of color are not the majority of homeowners and this becomes the underlying issue of funding for poor school districts. Historically, Black, Indigenous, and People of Color (BIPOC) are the ones who are severely impacted by the 10th Amendment and the powers reserved to the state government with regards to education. Not having access to resources is not a new discovery; it is the daily lives of children of color. Since the early foundations of the United States, education has been used as a tool to separate and categorize students based on their race, gender, sex, and geographic location. We must acknowledge the systemic laws that were created to prevent Black, Indigenous, and People of Color from succeeding in this world.

Providing equity through teaching online can realistically be tackled if educators first acknowledge there are disparities that exist in education. Equity online involves teachers considering the lack of access to technology many students have and creating multiple pathways that enable students to engage, collaborate, and make connections like their counterparts. Equity is fully understanding that you cannot rely on a system that has failed children of color for over 400 years to provide access and a quality education for all.

One example of what could be done is to create a PBL task that enables all learners to target the same standard but submit different products. It may seem a bit difficult, but in order for you to truly display equity, you must provide different paths for students to target standards. Most recently, I shared the "Identity" project. This PBL asked students to dig deep into their history and relate it to today. It challenged students to analyze just how much their identity is shaped by their experiences (whether they are positive or negative). They were also asked to compare how artists from the 1920s and 2020 used their experiences and identities to create works of art. This allowed students to reflect on their own identity and how the killings of Breonna Taylor and George Floyd have changed or confirmed their beliefs about the world around them.

Another aspect of teaching for equity online is knowing which learning management systems (LMS) or platforms to use. This entails understanding the concept that "not everything that glitters is gold." A student's learning ability is as unique as a birthmark. No two children learn the same way, which an educator should always keep in mind when deciding which platforms to use. The decision to use platforms should always be based on the concept of differentiation. Which platforms are designed for your below, at level, and above level learners? Equity is evident when platforms that are chosen can readily be accessed, effectively used, and relevant to all students. "It is learning how to take our differences and make them strengths. For the master's tools will never dismantle the master's house" (Lorde, 1984, p. 2).

Some platforms that can be used to ensure equity in your physical classroom and online are Flipgrid, Nearpod, and Wakelet. All three platforms are beneficial to all of your learners. One example of how Flipgrid can be used to teach for equity is by allowing students to voice their opinions, thoughts, or concerns through video features and also a blackboard feature. I created a "Back to the Future" PBL where students were asked to think about events that had occurred in the past and choose ways they would share this information in the future. What is most exciting about Flipgrid is you can use other applications or platforms with it. For this project students used Storyboard That, Google Slides, iMovie, and Adobe Spark with Flipgrid to create a letter of advice, museum exhibit, song, or short scripted movie. I encouraged students to use whichever project idea resonated with them the most. What I found out was that my students were very creative and some had even blended two project ideas into one.

Equity is not only about ensuring students have technological tools. It is ensuring students can make connections with what you are teaching. Students are able to resonate with products you are asking them to complete and students have a sense of meaningful collaboration with not only their classmates, but with you as the teacher.

Inclusion

Teaching online enables educators to use effective resources that challenge how our students think and learn, while also assessing needs such as cultural relevance and inclusion. Inclusion in a physical classroom space involves the pedagogue knowing their student. Though this sounds like common sense, the reality is that most educators don't. Knowing your student goes beyond knowing their name, which took you a week to remember, or knowing their transcripts, which is probably the first thing you look at when a student answers questions incorrectly in your class. Inclusion is recognizing the unique differences every student possesses that can be used to cultivate a thriving classroom community. A way in which you can learn those unique differences is by taking the time to get to know your students.

The online experience is a bit challenging for most educators and students alike. It forces both stakeholders to climb out of their comfort zones and learn new ways of teaching and learning. The positive impact of this experience is the ability for the educator to provide multiple avenues for students to obtain and critically analyze information. Students will have multiple forms of finding, experimenting, and making connections with discovered answers. For all to work simultaneously, an educator must first consider all students when planning curricula, lessons, and most importantly class activities. Who your students are, their learning styles, and where they come from should always dictate what you create for them to engage with in your remote/physical classroom. It also should dictate the feedback you provide for students that promote academic success and an assessment of the "how" and "why" of learning.

Although suddenly teaching online has caused much confusion with education and the disparities that exist within education, one must reflect on what inclusion looks like for all learners. Regardless of a learners abilities, disabilities, or healthcare needs, they have the right to an adequate education that fosters academic growth and cultivates a sense of acknowledgement. This is truly seen through feedback teachers give students on work. Teaching for inclusion online requires educators to fully comprehend how critical giving actionable feedback is to every learner. Your feedback online should be used as a form of data. Once you comment on student work, you should review it to see what changes need to be made to assignments (to help meet the needs of your students). If you notice that most of your students are struggling in the same area, perhaps you can revisit the assignment and take a look at what needs to be changed; this can be something as easy as certain vocabulary words being used. This feedback data you have given students should then be used to drive your instruction. Inclusion is ensuring that at every step of your lesson, you are providing space for reflection and next steps for students. This could be done on your Google Classroom, Google Hangouts, or even directly on the assignment. Your feedback guides a student's learning, thus encouraging them to engage in your classroom and have a sense of worth.

Representation

Teaching for representation online encourages teachers to use tools that reflect students' interests, race, community, and most important their learning style. What tools have you used to engage all learners in a way that represents who they are as individuals? How have you included students in the learning process?

An educator has to be willing to become experts of platforms, this way the learning experience can be tailored to the direct needs, learning styles, and preferences of students. One must also consider the benefits of using an online platform. Many benefits of using an online platform include immersive reader, integration of videos, and also blackboard features. These benefits are all examples of how to teach for representation online.

When planning for students who are below level or an English language learner, educators tend to provide avenues of differentiated text, instructions, and also provide onsite one-on-one assistance. Through the use of the right online platform (specific for your own students), students are able to use immersive readers to access the same assistance you once provided in person. The difference is that you are preparing your low-level students to become independent thinkers. In this instance, representation is providing the means for students to teach themselves, with platforms that are of interest to them.

When planning for your approaching, at level, or above level students, it is important to remember that videos can be used as a reinforcement of content and strategies. Videos can also be used as a substitute to introduce new content to students in place of a mini lecture. Where you might have spent time with these learners in class placing these learners in small groups, embedding videos into your lessons online provides the same support, while encouraging students to find their own videos as well. The online platform that you choose should be one that encourages independence and research skills.

The school building is an escape for most students. It is how they can break away from their current living situations and be seen as "normal" to their counterparts. Teaching for representation online should always include students who fear sharing their living situations with others. Finding the appropriate tools to address this issue means searching for a platform that enables a blackboard feature. The blackboard/whiteboard feature allows students to engage in content, activities, and class participation without having to consider showing where they live or how they live. While using Flipgrid, students were able to use the blackboard feature to display what they had learned, but did not have to share their personal living conditions. Your lessons or planning of your lessons should always include this option. As a teacher, you will want to create a lesson that gives students the option to use the blackboard/whiteboard feature instead of showing their face or homes as the background in videos. Incorporate that option in your instructions, this way students do not feel as if they are being singled out. Prior to announcing to students that they can use the whiteboard feature, you can create a Flipgrid Shorts video displaying for students how to use the whiteboard/blackboard feature properly. Representation is acknowledging that not all students live in current situations that should be shared with the world.

A final example of teaching for representation online is the use of choice boards of ideas. A choice board of ideas is a graphic organizer that allows students to choose from various products options to discuss content that has been learned. The advantage of creating choice boards is that you are providing different ways for your learners to display their understanding. Not all students are great at writing. By providing choices for students, such as create a summary, song, video, slideshow, comic book strip, or meme, you are differentiating learning in your classroom and showing that you understand your students. This takes us back to culturally responsive teaching. By creating choice boards, you are simplifying lesson planning and addressing learner interests.

The online experience with choice boards is great. The freedom of choice allows students to take ownership of their chosen work and fosters independence. Choice board ideas do not necessarily need to be in a specific order. The best advice is not to give students more than nine choices to choose from. Some educators have used the "Tic-Tac-Toe" strategy, where students can choose up to three products, activities, or readings to complete, while others simply display the choices, and students are instructed to choose one or two product ideas from the board. While using an online choice board, you can incorporate direct links to the apps you may want students to use for the particular activity or even HyperDocs that will take students to the next step of the project. Either way, accessibility and accountability are evident when using choice boards online.

The United States is realizing its deficiency in providing a sound education, granted by the US Constitution, for all children. Prior to remote learning, the inequities in education were prevalent but many ignored the visible structures that were of benefit to the rich and wealthy. With a newfound dependence on technology, the Department of Education has now noticed how many students in low socioeconomic communities are without resources. With the staggering numbers of family households who are without technology or resources, one has to question legislation. It is safe to say that they too believe the nation would be better off not adequately funding education and allowing students of color to fall further behind the learning gap. If this is so, how will underserved children ever meet the demands of a 21st-century job?

Teaching for equity, inclusion, and representation online should always involve students. Involving students includes using platforms your students are used to, creating culturally responsive tasks, and most importantly creating opportunities for students to make connections with their communities and outside world. There is no perfect way to teach, but there is a perfect way to show students their worth, and that is by considering all of the diverse individuals that are watching you from their cell phones, iPads, and computers at home. Be cognizant of your audience—as you would prefer to be recognized for your unique differences, students would like to be as well. Let us put an end to reminding students of trauma and be better at reminding them of how successful and great their ancestors were. Learn about the success of the diverse identities in your remote learning classroom, incorporate it into your teaching, and see how different and engaging your curricula becomes.

References

Brown v. Board of Education of Topeka, 347 U.S. 483. (1954). (n.d.). Retrieved from Justia US Supreme Court: https://supreme.justia.com/cases/federal/us/347/483/

Lorde, A. (1984). The master's tools will never dismantle the master's house (Sister Outsider: Essays and Speeches) (pp. 110–114). Berkeley, CA: Crossing Press.

Robinson, K. (2010, October). Changing education paradigms. TED: Ideas Worth Spreading. Retrieved from www.ted.com/talks/sir_ken_robinson_changing_education_paradigms

9

Social-Emotional Learning in an Online/Blended Environment

Gloria Cazarez

Introduction

> Do the best you can until you know better. Then when
> you know better, do better.
> —Maya Angelou

I preface this chapter with the timeless words of Maya Angelou because we're at a historical point in time within the realm of education where there are many opportunities for us to improve on our practice as educators and community leaders. We stand on the precipice of what has been and what could be. Educators, administrators, and families have all been launched into the unknown. Through the various crises that we've faced and continue to face, there's an opportunity to do better, as Ms. Angelou shared. What has traditionally been social-emotional learning (SEL) can be reimagined due to the unique circumstances we're in. As a teacher, I've had flexibility in what and how I teach that I never had before due to emergency remote teaching. As a site and community, we put our students and their families first. In meetings, we're asked by administrators for input on how we could best attend to the "whole child" and meet their SEL needs first through remote teaching. As we return to a different version of what schooling has looked like, let's not forget the value in SEL.

Why SEL?

SEL in the classroom is nothing new to most of us in the field. In 1994, the term was originally coined by the Collaborative to Advance Social Emotional Learning (CASEL) organization (Core SEL, 2020). Since then, SEL refers to

> the process through which children and adults understand and manage emotions, set and achieve positive goals, feel and show empathy for others, establish and maintain positive relationships, and make responsible decisions.
>
> (Core SEL, 2020)

At the time, researchers were exploring emotional skills in the classroom and how to improve students' emotional competence as they went about their academic school day. The five core competencies within SEL that are typically fostered are *self-awareness*, *self-management*, *social awareness*, *relationship skills*, and *responsible decision making* (Core SEL, 2020). Good SEL curriculum will include lessons and activities that address most of these, but a meaningful SEL curriculum is created when you adapt these lessons to meet the needs of the learners in your class that year.

Whether it's the historical civil rights protests around the world through #BlackLivesMatter, political turmoil, or the collective trauma incurred by the effects of a pandemic, we can all feel the weight of the world on our shoulders every day. Our learners are coming to us with the same weight or more, as their understandings and experiences may highly differ from ours. The child who used to worry about which friends to play with at morning recess may now be worried about hearing her parents discuss the rent, job loss, or both. The child whose parents rely on school for child care has many more worries in his mind than learning how the bossy "e" rule works. If we have hundreds of questions about what our teaching future looks like, we can be sure that our learners are coming to us with thousands more and we will not have concrete answers. These concerns need to be addressed in order for us to successfully attend to the actual academic part of education. These stressors don't live in a backpack that magically stays home when the morning bell rings. Our students need to know that their feelings are valid and normal considering the circumstances we're in. They need to be explicitly told that they're not alone. We understand that their families are struggling financially, socially, emotionally, and physically, and we are here for them. We hear the anxieties they're coming in with, we see them, and we acknowledge them. As one of my favorite TED Talks speakers, Linda Cliatt-Wayman, once said, "So what? Now what?"

Now, we reflect on what we know and take actionable steps towards creating a welcoming environment despite the challenges that we will inevitably face. If you're a fan of morning meetings from the Responsive Classroom like myself, they don't need to stop because we've been tasked with transitioning to hybrid teaching. Morning meetings can still occur through 15–20 minutes of Zoom or Google Meet time. They can be extended and made more interactive by using a weekly grid on Flipgrid where students can respond to a weekly SEL prompt and reply to one another. At the start of every school year, we begin with getting to know you (GTKY) and community building activities because we see it as an investment in the long run. This doesn't need to be dropped because the school year may look different and can simply be adjusted to meet our specific needs. Now is a great time to ask ourselves the tough questions. *How am I fostering self-awareness in the classroom? What routines are in place that practice social awareness and self-management?* Whether we're in a brick-and-mortar class or digital space, fostering the social and emotional development of our learners and intentionally teaching coping strategies will help them thrive as they grow in a shared environment. Part of the magic in SEL tools and practices is that they become an active part of how we go about our daily lives; how we react, what words we choose, and how we take on challenging moments.

BYOTB: Build Your Own Tool Belt

While we understand and see the value in taking the time to attend to our students' SEL needs through in-class activities, education as we know it is changing week by week. *How can this be implemented in a hybrid model of instruction? Or a fully remote-teaching model? How will I assist my learner at the calm corner in my room while maintaining physical distancing?* There won't be any clear cut answers in this chapter, but there are some helpful hints and strategies that have worked in my classroom and a few others I've worked with.

Flower Tool

Description

The flower tool came about when a student of mine shared with me that when he's very angry or very sad, his mom asked him to *smell the flower, and put out the candle.* Later, I found that it's a well-known mindfulness strategy used by therapists, parents, and teachers, that asks a child to take a deep breath by closing his/her eyes and envisioning themselves smelling a flower, then blowing out a birthday candle. Envisioning the actions in a context that makes sense for our learners is often beneficial in the effectiveness of this coping strategy. In Figure 9.1 you can see a Google slide with two halved-sections. The first section has the writing/thinking prompt, "How can you use the flower tool today?" with a textbox left empty for student response. The second section has a large image of the flower tool.

Hula-Hoop Tool

Description

One of the constant conflicts in the K-6 arena is often personal space, or rather the lack of it between our learners. Which is why it's one of the first things that my grade level addresses at the start of the year. Using a hula-hoop, or sometimes it's referred

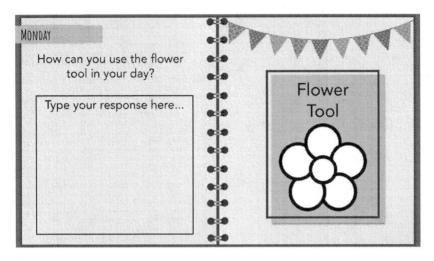

FIGURE 9.1 Google Slide—SEL journaling.

Source: Image created by Gloria Cazarez © 2020

to as a *space bubble*, has been common practice for years within education. From August through June I find myself repeating "Hula-hoop, Marcos!" as I see him about to grab his best friend by the shoulders at line-up. With the possibility of returning to a classroom space with the current health concerns, explicitly teaching about personal space and physical distancing is essential.

Hammer Tool

Description

The hammer tool we use in reference to something strong and powerful like a hammer, which in this case is the power of our words. Within the SEL world, clear communication is essential in getting what you need. This can be true for ourselves as teachers or for our students during their school day. When conflicts arose between students, they often needed to practice clear communication. I would gently remind them, "Could your hammer tool help right now?" Sometimes the response was a quick nod, or a begrudging "I guess . . ." and usually it helped diffuse a situation that could have easily escalated. Helping our students identify and use words like *overwhelmed*, *frustrated*, or *sad* to communicate with others is an invaluable life skill.

Bin Tool

Description

The bin tool was created out of the countless minor issues that come up in the average student's day. When a peer may say that the color green is for losers, I usually advise them to use the bin and toss the words away. This tool is for those small problems that are often exacerbated within our students' perspective, that simply need to be thrown away in the garbage bin. People will say mean things or harmful words, and sometimes we can just choose to not give them any power. I want to be clear that I'm not advocating for the use of this strategy within the context of bullying, or repetitive targeting. This would not be the route we take when students use harmful actions or language based on gender, sexual orientation, culture, or ethnic backgrounds. Using the bin tool has helped my students in various scenarios both in class and at home. I do ask them to use their bin tool in situations that aren't as urgent or harmful as others. There was no lasting harm done, verbal or physical, and they can choose to go on with their day.

Implementation

Introducing these coping strategies and implementing them can vary and I encourage you to adapt this to make it fit your specific needs. As with most lessons, I usually:

- ◆ Introduce the strategy through a read-aloud or real example.
- ◆ Explicitly discuss appropriate scenarios.
- ◆ Model the use together.

♦ Create and share (writing prompt, sketch, poster, journal, skit, video, etc.).

Online Adaptations

If we're being tasked with teaching online, I'm envisioning a large variety of options by incorporating these tools within the digital classroom space. Use can vary depending on what LMS your district is using or what platforms you and your students are comfortable with.

Flipgrid

Thanks to the interactivity and easy-to-use tools on Flipgrid, embedding these SEL skills can be easier than expected. You can create one grid to teach each tool and ask for student responses based on relevant prompts such as *How can you use the flower tool in your day? Has there been a time when the flower tool could have helped you or someone you know?* This platform allows our students to see and hear each other's replies, while also engaging with one another. The extra features within Flipgrid, such as sticky notes, emojis, and stickers, allow for student personalities to shine through a digital space.

Google Classroom/Slides

Whether you've been using Google Classroom or recently transitioned into it, it's also a great way of sharing content and lessons with your learners. In the past, I have recorded myself reading a book to launch the tool, and shared that video to our Google Classroom feed. I would also create a slide deck, with a journaling theme that asks students similar prompts along with matching clipart: *Tell me about a time when someone respected or disrespected your personal space at school? In class? How could the hula-hoop or hammer tool help?* What's neat about assigning a slide deck to each student is that they each get their own copy and only you as the instructor sees their responses. If students want to share their thoughts, they can always post on the main Google Classroom feed.

More SEL Tools for Your Teacher Tool Belt

Digital Calm Corner on Google Slides

To specifically attend to my learners' SEL needs during emergency remote teaching, I had to adapt on the fly and make something work. Browsing through many teacher blogs dealing with the same issue, I found a creative way of still having a calm corner digitally. Using Google Slides, I created a short guide for my learners to use, in moments that they would typically visit our in-class calm corner. Below you can find a sample of what guiding questions are on the slides.

♦ How big is your problem (on a scale of 1–3)?
♦ How are you feeling right now? (Identify and name your emotions.)
♦ What coping skills do you want to try?

There are many creative and talented teachers out there, so a quick Google search for "digital calm corner" will give you many results to choose from or be inspired by. I prefer making my own version to personalize it based on what my learners that year need, but again, do what works for you. In Figure 9.2

FIGURE 9.2 *How big is the problem you're facing?* Interactive slide.

Source: Image created by Gloria Cazarez © 2020

there is a landscape image of three mountains that get higher as you look at them from left to right. There is a question prompt and a cloud at the top left. The image is from an interactive slide where students are asked to identify how big their problem is as they work their way through an SEL slide deck via Google Classroom.

Emotional Regulation and Check-ins on Jamboard

Establishing a foundation for identifying emotions and balancing them is always a challenge for many reasons. There's either never enough time in our day or it requires prep, but addressing emotions can happen in a hybrid teaching world. Some teachers may be expected to host a daily synchronous meeting, and that's when you can use an emotions check-in as a starter. While allowing the first three to five minutes for all participants to join your meet, you can have a shared Jamboard open for students to move their labeled note to the feeling they currently identify with. Figure 9.3 is an image of an SEL Google Jamboard students can collaboratively share on. It has a range of emojis that represent various emotions on a spectrum from left to right. The Jamboard has students' names on sticky-notes so they can each move their sticky-note to whichever emoji matches their current emotions. At the end, teachers can ask if any students want to share out with their peers.

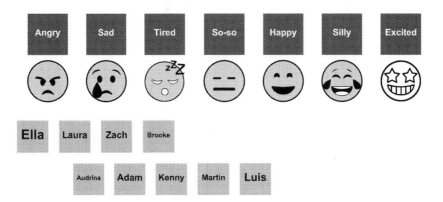

FIGURE 9.3 Emotions check-in via Jamboard.

Source: Image created by Gloria Cazarez © 2020

Social and Emotional Check-ins on Flipgrid

In-class, asynchronous, or synchronous check-ins with our students will continue to be key as we try to navigate hybrid learning models. In class, we would have our morning meeting every day where we addressed an SEL tool or a new coping skill. Virtually, the same activity can be achieved through Flipgrid, Jamboard, or Padlet. When we had to transition to remote teaching, I created a weekly grid via Flipgrid where I asked for student responses and provided them with supportive feedback. One week it was simple prompts like, *What has been your favorite activity to do at home?* Other weeks it was related back to our SEL tools: *Have you needed to use your flower breaths since distance learning started? Did you use any of our other tools to help you get through a tough time?* Daily check-ins with our learners go a long way in creating environments where they're equipped with the necessary tools to thrive in the classroom.

Culturally Sustaining Lens

We teach what we value.
—Gloria Ladson-Billings

Considering this distinctive moment in time that we find ourselves in, why not also use this as a chance to revamp our practice? When we look at how we approach SEL in real life or online, we can add on a culturally sustaining lens to our teaching tool belt that can address worldly events that are affecting our communities. Gaining this new perspective on how we teach asks us to look into culturally sustaining pedagogy which "seeks to perpetuate and foster linguistic, literate, and cultural aspects as a part of schooling for positive social transformation in our classrooms" (Paris & Alim, 2017).

Every year we are tasked with doing what's right for our students and in regards to SEL, we are asked to teach the whole child. In these times, we cannot teach the whole child if we ignore what they come in with: their culture, language, values, interests, and assets. We aren't attending to the whole child, while we may demean and criticize the rich backgrounds and cultures that they bring into our classroom communities. This means not only recognizing binary/non-binary genders within our spaces but creating an environment where accepting language is normative through routines and embedded practices. This means having open and healthy discussions on why Black lives not only matter, but deserve to thrive in a system that has yet to be built. Our families are calling on us to transform our often deficit-based mindsets into asset-based ones that celebrate the rich diversity we can find within the confines of our spaces.

In Practice

A lot of ground can be covered during those first few weeks of GTKY lessons and we keep what needs continued practice. Depending on what's appropriate for your grade levels, there are several approaches to foster a culturally sustaining space. Here are a few of them:

- ◆ Decenter yourself/recenter your learners
- ◆ Inclusive introductions
- ◆ We are all teachers; we are all learners

Decenter Yourself/Recenter Your Learners

This practice can happen both in the classroom and outside, on our own time. In order to put our learners and their needs first, we need to start by acknowledging what we're bringing in our invisible knapsack when we enter the classroom. What privileges, triggers, and experiences do we have? How can we be open and have discussions about this with our students? How can we recenter them and what they bring to the table?

The conversation can be initiated with students as young as 1st grade, about what privileges are and what privileges they can identify with. Some sample questions can be: *Did your parents go to college? Do you have a stay-at-home parent? Is there a grocery store with fresh fruits and veggies near your home?* Where sample questions for middle and high schoolers may look a lot more age-appropriate, such as: *Have you ever thought twice about calling the police when you encounter a conflict? Could you travel to most places in your country and feel safe?* In making this more culturally sustaining and asset-based, we can ask questions that place value on our diverse backgrounds such as: *Do you speak more than one language? Are you aware of the history of generational family members (great-grandparents, grandparents)? Do you know how to find foods/spices that are special to your culture? Do you celebrate events that may not be widely known to others in the community?*

Using the ever-popular anchor chart paper or a virtual whiteboard like Google's Jamboard, you can document your own and your students' growth in this area. Once we identify what privileges we have, we can use them to help others who may not be as fortunate. If you have a student who speaks one or more languages, how can that student now use that asset to help others? This can be as simple as sharing a read aloud in class or recording themselves on Flipgrid sharing the richness of another language.

Inclusive Introductions

As we continue to learn about best practices in our classrooms and being more culturally responsive to our communities' needs, it should go without saying that this includes the LGBTQIA+ community. Inclusive read alouds with main characters from diverse backgrounds, two moms, two dads, and so many others are part of making sure that all of our learners feel welcome and acknowledged in the classroom. Having a discussion about gender stereotypes and assumptions can come naturally as a boy may be heard exclaiming, "You can't like blue, Mrs. C, that's a boy color!" or a girl may be telling a friend, "Purple glitter pencils aren't for boys, Grey." We'd be lying to ourselves if we claim these comments haven't been shared within our spaces. Once enough conversation and discussion has occurred with you as a guide, you can start incorporating self-identified pronouns in basic introductions, if the individuals feel safe enough to share. It's not our job to initiate or force anyone to *out* themselves or put anyone on the spot. Our goal should be to make our shared spaces inclusive of all the identities we serve, and make it so preferred pronouns can be embedded as a normative practice.

We're All Teachers, We're All Learners

While I keep referring to the students in our space as *learners*, they've often taught me much more than what I taught them. There have been times when I start the lesson with a target standard(s) to hit, and our class discussion, guided by their questions, end up covering bigger, all-encompassing themes. Other times, we simply need to make the tools, time, and flexibility available and step away. Whoever is doing the most work is doing the actual learning. Here are a few areas in which we as teachers can benefit from taking a backseat and being a learner:

♦ Name pronunciation
♦ Deficit mindset approach
♦ Demeaning dialects
♦ Assumptions and stereotypes of family structures and immigrant status

Being guilty of using harmful language within all of those areas myself, I know I can do better. I can take the time to learn how to pronounce their names and last names correctly. There's so much power in a name and their names come with an important story that needs to be shared. I want my students to leave my class knowing that their names are important and there's value in that. While there are several examples of a deficit mindset approach, a common one is the use of the term "English language learner" (ELL), which centers the western colonial perspective and value of the English language. A refreshing approach I've learned the past few years is using the term "emergent bilingual learner" (EBL) as coined by Ofelia Garcia. This puts the emphasis on bilingualism as a positive trait or an asset, versus focusing on the lack of the English language.

Another area in which I often need to remind myself to do better is in recognizing the complexity and value in using varying dialects of English, Spanish, and other languages. Many times we may bring in our own judgement on what proper English is and shame our students for their use of African American Vernacular English (AAVE) in the classroom. My own Mexican

American family doesn't speak proper Spanish or Castilian Spanish because that's not the world we grew up in. We learned to speak a local, Americanized version of Spanish that's spoken in our area of California. It's okay for us to not know or be familiar in these varieties, but it's never okay to assume their lesser than because it's different.

Lastly, there are the times when we bring in our own values and beliefs to our roles as educators in diverse spaces. The families that entrust their children to us deserve for us to serve the different family structures without our personal judgment causing harm. It's 2020 and we will have parents who identify as part of the LGBTQIA+ community, we will have single parent households, and we will have parents or guardians who are immigrants. Our job isn't to belittle them or reinforce destructive stereotypes in an environment that's supposed to support them. Our job is to engage, listen, learn, and amplify their voices as active participants in our school community.

Magic in Malleability

We got into teaching because our hearts belong in the classroom; we want to give back to a community that has given so much to us and build towards a better future. However, we've remained in teaching because we've learned how to innovate and adapt on the fly. Teachers are forced to innovate when our site budgets are slashed and we adapt when changes in legislation or testing directly impact how and what we teach. While teaching through a pandemic is no one's ideal scenario, it's where we are and we can find the silver linings in that. Districts and states found funds to ensure most of our families had internet access and devices at home. Communication between school and home has improved drastically, out of necessity to simply connect with one another during the COVID-19 crisis. Volunteers within our communities have stepped up to make sure school lunches are still available to those who are in need. EdTech companies also did their part by opening free subscriptions to teachers and families, knowing that we were all in a tough situation. The ability for all of us to bend a bit without breaking got us through the end of the 2019–2020 school year, and that's pretty impressive considering what we were facing.

It's a tough realization for any educator, including myself, that there is no going back to *how things were*. Most of our districts are exploring three options for the start of the school year: in-class (at-site with social distancing), a hybrid model (at-site and online), or distance learning (online/remote teaching). Now more than ever, it's important for us to remain flexible in our expectations of learners and of ourselves. If a morning meeting was an essential part of my teaching day, how can I plan for it to happen online? How will it be different, similar, or better? Even if I'm told to start teaching in the classroom in August, who's to say that won't change when flu season comes along? This is why our ability to be able to provide our learners with an enriching educational experience regardless of where we physically teach is so important. I'm going into the start of the school year with an open mind, an open heart, and knowing that I am able to build upon the SEL strategies and practices in my teacher tool belt to do what's right by my learners and the community I serve.

References

Core SEL Competencies. (2020, February 20). Retrieved June 16, 2020, from https://casel.org/core-competencies/

Paris, D., & Alim, H. S. (2017). *Culturally sustaining pedagogies: Teaching and learning for justice in a changing world*. New York, NY: Teachers College Press.

10

Balancing the Home/School Connection

Hue-An Wren

So many factors mentioned in the previous chapters can posi-
tively impact student achievement when it comes to strategies for
remote learning. The home/school connection is just as vital to
the success of students. This key relationship should not be lost
when education shifts to a remote teaching and learning environment. The foundation built during the school year between
teacher and parent or guardian will be tested when instruction
shifts from in-person teaching to online. With the home environment being the primary learning space for students, teachers will
have to look at that connection differently in order to empower
students and facilitate effective learning environments.

This chapter explores the realities of students learning from
home and the many considerations teachers must make as they
try to continue the learning experience in an environment that
may not be as predictable as the school campus. Will there be
access to devices and high-speed internet? Will students have
support systems at home that help develop self-regulation
skills to maintain a steady learning routine? What support can
parents/guardians provide? How can teachers scaffold assignments and tasks to be both tech reliant as well as analog? What
support can the teacher provide families who are also learning

new skills at home? The processes and strategies adopted will need to take into consideration the community at large and readily available resources. The following narrative discusses the many considerations teachers must make when teaching from an online presence. Some considerations may not be accessible for a classroom teacher, but many will. The key is to focus on the purpose for these strategic considerations when focusing on student achievement and well-being.

Consideration #1: Scaffold the Learning

It is important to note that not all assignments will look the same when transitioning to an online space. Some students will need more support when shifting to digital assignments, especially if this was not the norm prior to moving to an online environment. Scaffolding assignments can manifest itself in a variety of ways. Adopting practices from the Universal Design for Learning guidelines can help make content more accessible to students considering their varied home environments. This is when parents and guardians in the home play a vital role in the student's success. Later in this chapter we dive deeper into the many roles parents and guardians play in this difficult balance of school and home. When teaching new content, consider offering videos for students who are learning while doing household chores. Try to ensure that videos have transcripts so that students who are unable to listen to videos can read the transcript if there is a sleeping sibling nearby. Audio recordings in the form of podcasts can be beneficial for students who prefer to listen while riding the bus, walking the dog, or any other household responsibility. Provide articles for students who prefer to slow down the content by reading. Providing articles can also be a teaching strategy that fosters critical thinking in reading and writing and may inevitably be beneficial for all students.

In an online environment, creating tutorials or how-to videos can prove to be effective for even the simplest tasks. This is the YouTube generation; if one doesn't know how to do something, it's likely that YouTube has a tutorial on how to do it. This generation of learners is highly visual and values the inherent convenience of a tutorial. This would be an opportunity for teachers to create their own screencasts or tutorials. With the availability of cloud storage, these tutorials and screencasts can be saved into the cloud for students to access at their convenience. Many teachers choose to create websites that can act as resource hubs for lessons where students can go to find tutorials on topics that are being taught. Some teachers have even enlisted the support of other students or students from previous years to help create screencasts for their peers to be housed on the website. Often this task turns into an assignment where students create a screencast to demonstrate mastery. Students will get the experience of creating and learning to problem-solve as well as demonstrate mastery of content. Teachers benefit from having an engaging lesson as well as having a multitude of resources to choose from for next year's group of students.

In the beginning, the idea of creating resources seems daunting, but over time, the resources will accumulate and one can be assured that they will get better over time. These screencasts and tutorials can then become a resource for parents and guardians at home who are supporting the student's educational experience. Parents and guardians can look to these videos for clarification on instructions or to help students who may need a different explanation on the topic. Guardians can use the videos to learn on their own and then use that new learning to support the student.

Chunking lessons differently can help alleviate the burden of asynchronous learning for families at home. When assigning chapters or lessons, extend deadlines so that families have time to get to the project. Six hours of in-person instruction does not equate to six hours of virtual learning, asynchronous or not. There are too many factors that affect the learning environment to think that a student would accomplish what he/she would accomplish in the same amount of seat time in class. Students who are not as self-motivated as others will then rely on parents or guardians to help stay motivated. Longer deadlines will alleviate much of the pressure on families. Consider that a project will take longer in a virtual classroom and that will allow your students to come back with better quality work.

Consideration #2: Provide Support for Parents/Guardians

There is always a learning curve when new technology is introduced to the classroom. Add that to the already overwhelming circumstances that families need to cope with and you get a frustrating situation for both student and parent. Technology moves so quickly, and it is not easy for parents to keep up with all of the tools being used in the classroom. Screencasts or tutorials on how to submit an assignment into the learning management system (LMS) may seem overly simple, but this may be the first time a parent has seen this type of interaction in education. Remember that it took weeks to introduce routines and structures to students at the beginning of the school year. This may also be the case when you set routines and structures for your virtual classroom. Students will need to learn these skills as well as the parents and guardians. Younger students will rely on their parents and guardians to help address technical difficulties. Addressing these technical difficulties ahead of time by providing step-by-step instructions can help alleviate the concerns parents may have.

When introducing a new digital tool, make sure it is inherently clear how to access or use that tool. Communicate with your students and their parents or guardians what apps will need to be installed, how to access certain tools on different devices, and what permissions and accounts will need to be created. During in-person classes, if the school had 1:1 devices for students, the teacher could depend on a certain level of predictability when it came to what device is being used, what operating systems are embedded, and what filters are placed on the network. This predictability makes it easy for teachers to know what technical difficulties students may encounter and be able to troubleshoot it. When education shifts to remote learning, students can be using a variety of devices and will need support from parents to help them access the content and assignments. For teachers who are comfortable with technology, it is easy to tinker and play with the software until we have a solid understanding of how it works. The situation may be different for your students' guardians. Depending on age, socioeconomic circumstances, and a variety of other external influences, many guardians may not have been exposed to technology until it ended up in their child's hands. This may be the perfect time to open those tutorials and screencasts to the community as well. Make one-page documents that are translated and easy to understand from someone who does not come from an education background. In the end, students are looking to their parents when they need to troubleshoot and there is no more helpless feeling than to not be able to help your child.

Consideration #3: Have Family Nights

Take this opportunity to build relationships with your students' families. Guardians will be more involved in student learning in an online setting and the percentage of involvement increases exponentially the younger the age of the students. By hosting family nights as school functions, teachers can take this time to teach valuable skills and give parents a chance to ask questions that they may not have been able to do so before. Family nights can center around a subject, a skill, or even a holiday celebration. Family nights that focus on technology give teachers a chance to teach guardians how to use the tools that students use in their virtual classrooms now. Focusing on concepts like STEAM (Science, Technology, Engineering, Art, and Math) skills gives families something to take away that lets them continue the learning after family night. Use this opportunity to demonstrate tools that are being used in the classroom as well as build relationships within the community. This will give parents and guardians a chance to connect with others so that they can build their network. This network will be valuable in a time when it feels like we are all feeling isolated at home.

Consideration #4: Teach Self-Regulation Skills

Many of the procedures and policies set up in our classrooms are designed to help students succeed. A student isn't tardy to class because there is an inherent disciplinary action associated with tardiness. A student continues to turn in homework because the teacher checks the work every day. Each step of the writing process is separated so that students complete one chunk at a time before moving on to the next. Students have support systems for emotional and academic challenges everywhere they turn. All of these routines have been set in place to ensure that students succeed. But what if there is nothing in place that helps a student stay on track with projects? Who will be there when challenges arise to model calming reactions and behavior? What emotional coping and time management skills do educators assume our students have? Have students had ample practice regulating work ethic and project management? In a delicate balance of synchronous and asynchronous work, do students have the time management skills to ensure that progress is made on assignments each day? Parents and guardians are now taking on the responsibility of making sure students continue to be supported.

To help ease this transition, maintain communication with support systems at home to answer questions and provide insight on academic obstacles students may have. Make deadlines for assignments longer than usual. Embedding a daily or weekly calendar as a central hub for students to check every day helps students who lack organizational skills. This hub can be used to link assignments, tutorials, help documents, or pertinent information for lessons. Minimize opportunities for confusion and that will set students up for success.

Using an LMS can also help students stay organized so they can find all resources and assignments in one central location. In a remote learning environment, students can be faced with numerous distractions and organizing materials ahead of time for them can help alleviate an already overwhelming experience. Self-regulatory skills can also be reinforced with constant feedback. Offer projects that allow students to have ongoing feedback. This will give students a chance to learn from their mistakes and submit work that is truly representative of what they are capable of. Try to stay on top of the formative feedback so that students grow from your advice.

Teachers can also look to foster effective study skills into lessons. Especially as students get older, a teacher may assume that having access to a study guide will give students the ability to prepare for exams. It is often the case that students have no idea how to use a study guide to "study." What does studying look like? How does one use this study guide to prepare for assessments? Model what studying looks like by creating those steps into a homework assignment. As students are doing their homework, they find that they are, in fact, studying for their exams. Strategies that ask students to memorize facts are better suited for gamified learning in digital platforms that quiz students, resulting in a much more fun environment. Many web-based quizzing platforms offer single sign-on for education domains and the ability to create classes for accountability. Look for platforms that offer live game play as well as student-paced practice for scaffolding. Students who need more support can gain access to these games before the teacher starts a live session. This ensures success for students who may not do well in a competitive environment and as they find small pockets of time, they can continue to practice on their own. Encourage group work and collaboration for both synchronous and asynchronous work. Giving students opportunities to work with their peers allows them to practice those self-regulation skills. Invite parents and guardians to observe presentations and group work. This gives them an inside view of what you're expecting of the student.

For academic support, ask students to review work in a cyclical pattern so that they are reviewing as well as learning new material. This type of review can help students as they prepare for final assessments where they will need to retrieve information learned earlier in the term. This can also be embedded into assignments where a teacher requires students to practice the new skill as well as answer some review questions from previous lessons. This will keep those previous lessons fresh in their minds so that the knowledge is easily retrievable when it is time to take the exams. Many of these strategies can be embedded in the way an assignment is crafted. A well-crafted lesson will teach students more than just the content. It will teach the many skills needed for success later in college and career. Balancing both emotional and academic support can help students learn to regulate emotions in an environment that can be isolating.

Consideration #5: Account for the Home Environment

Success in an online environment can be affected by a variety of external factors that may or may not be noticeable to those outside the student's home. How can students be responsible for classwork when there are other factors demanding their attention? Is the student taking care of siblings in addition to trying to get homework done? Is the student working a part-time job to help offset the loss of wages due to business shutdowns? Many digital tools include a timestamp for student submissions. If a student is submitting work late in the evening or early in the day, consider the possibility that there are other family obligations that may be more pressing at the moment. If so, how can assignments be organized in a way that is manageable for a student who may be balancing other duties? Consider chunking assignments so that small chunks can be completed a little at a time. Having extended due dates on assignments or allowing alternate assignments can help alleviate some of the pressures associated with balancing the demands of home as well as school.

Home environments may also be the reason for spotty attendance in synchronous sessions. If students are caring for siblings at home, meeting for class at 10AM may not be a feasible option. For younger students, parents who are also working from home may not be able to help students attend synchronous sessions during the day. Value that synchronous time spent with students and make sure that it is worth their time. It took a lot for a family to get the device, the internet connection, and the dedicated time and space to be able to get to your video conference. If your lesson can be completed with a screencast or a tutorial, save it for asynchronous lessons. Spend the synchronous sessions addressing misconceptions, building relationships, sparking engagement, and checking for understanding of content.

If a student isn't attending synchronous sessions regularly, consider alternative ways to deliver the content. Screencasts and tutorials work well accompanied by digital platforms that embed accountability. Asynchronous activities can offer students a way to engage with the content on their own time. Make sure the content that you deliver is meaningful and engaging. With

YouTube at their disposal, students can learn anything anytime they want. What is motivating them to learn with you? Consider offering real-world applications with the concepts that you teach. Their lives are more embedded into schooling than it's ever been before. Now is the time to capitalize on all the teachable moments that happen at home. Differentiation of content can also help students who may not be motivated to attend sessions. Consider multiple means of representation from the Universal Design for Learning guidelines in the content you deliver as well as the product they turn in to demonstrate mastery. Empowering students to choose how they want to demonstrate mastery will give them control in a seemingly chaotic time. Choice boards that offer both digital and analog projects can address many of the concerns that affect student success in an online environment. Many choice boards start off small, with one or two options for students to choose from, but over time, as new tools are introduced, the board can grow and students can have a variety of tools to choose from. Collaborate with colleagues across your school and the options on the choice board will continue to grow exponentially over the course of the student's time in the school.

Consideration #6: Consider Student Access to Technology

Consider that devices may also be shared within a household as well. This may create technical problems with physical space, logging in and out of accounts, or wear and tear on the device itself. This is key when choosing a time for synchronous sessions or assigning asynchronous work with short windows for completion. Consider extending due dates for students who may need more time to work since they are sharing a device. Some school districts have been fortunate enough to provide devices for all students, but devices aren't very helpful if there is no internet to go with it. Access to the internet is still a growing problem and with so many cell phone plans with data, many homes choose to use the cell phone as their primary access to the internet instead of purchasing a wifi plan. While this may work for day-to-day interactions, school work may require more than what a cell phone can offer. Many cell phone companies and internet providers offer low-cost internet for qualifying candidates. Explore those resources and compile lists of resources for parents. Organize events where communities can learn how to access these resources together and invite local internet providers and cell phone companies.

Since a steady internet connection can be difficult to maintain, be considerate of the bandwidth of the content that is being shared in lessons. If a family is sharing a limited data plan, it may be difficult to stream media for video conferencing or watching tutorials. High-definition screencasts or tutorials may be difficult to view on a limited data plan. Consider creating lower-quality videos so that it doesn't take up as much bandwidth to view. Or consider chunking videos and making multiple screencasts or tutorials instead of one long one, so that students don't have to wait long for the video to buffer during intermittent internet connection. During video conferencing, consider allowing students to turn off the video to save bandwidth. Provide opportunities for students to do work offline and then upload it when the internet is available.

Consideration #7: Value the Parent-Teacher Relationship

Take time to build the relationship between teacher and parent. This can be valuable when a student is struggling. Parents and guardians can be allies when it comes to helping a student succeed. Reaching out to parents when a student is not attending synchronous sessions can help facilitate a conversation between parent and student about how to get back on track. Guardians can also be the guide on the side when learning new content. During lessons, both synchronous and asynchronous, parents and guardians can help clarify assignment instructions or help students contact the teacher for support. In distance education, your guardians are the ones who will troubleshoot the technology when it doesn't work properly and they will be the ones to make sure that students are getting access to the content that you teach. If a student can't figure out why the application isn't working, a parent can intervene to support or reach out for support.

Parents of very young students play an even bigger role. These students will need support during synchronous sessions as well as during asynchronous work. Logging on to a video conference call may be difficult for young children and navigating the computer during these calls is asking quite a bit of students, especially if this responsibility is new for them.

Parents and guardians of older students can help foster those much-needed self-regulatory skills so that students are prepared when they do come to class. For this reason, it is important to provide access to parents and guardians for screencasts or tutorials, as they may be watching as well so that they can help their children. They may be the ones who remind students that homework is due and that it is time to make progress on that large project. Value the time that they spend with their children and the balancing act that they may be doing with their own responsibilities in addition to supporting their child's learning. When you value what they are doing, what you assign students will be more meaningful and purposeful.

Consideration #8: Value Human Connections

In an online learning environment, communication and connection play an even bigger role in student success. This is the time to focus on connections. Connections between teacher and student, connections between teacher and parent, and the connections between student and student.

The connection between teacher and student sets the tone for the learning. When students have a connection with the teacher, they are more motivated to continue to do their best. They are more motivated to attend sessions and complete the work that is asked of them. Build on this relationship by offering feedback as often as possible. Feedback should be accompanied by the opportunity to do better and submit again. Videos and screencasts are also another way to add a personal feeling to content and assignments. Seeing the teacher creates a feeling of familiarity that is missing when suddenly shifting to an online environment.

The connection between parents and teacher is also vital to a student's success. When the teacher and parents have a strong connection, they work together as a team to help the student succeed in school. Teachers can communicate with parents when they notice a discrepancy in the student's work and parents can communicate with teachers when they need clarification or additional strategies for an assignment.

The connections between student and student are also vital to the social emotional well-being of the student. Humans are naturally gregarious and to be cut off from social interaction can be detrimental to one's emotional well-being. Students, especially high school students, are fiercely dependent on their friends. Consider offering opportunities for students to work on projects with their friends. This will not only bring much needed levity to a rather dismal situation, but it will also teach students how to collaborate in a digital space.

In a traditional in-person classroom setting, so much of the environment is controlled to ensure student success. Teachers post visual aides and motivational posters all over the walls to remind students to be diligent in their studies. Students move from class to class in a timely manner based on a very detailed schedule. Agendas and notes are posted in the classroom and teachers dedicate class time for students to write these down in school issued planners. Every morning, students hand in homework from the night before and they have opportunities in after-school clubs or libraries to get support when they need it. Even devices are managed so that accessing digital content is easier on the student.

But now, our students are no longer in the controlled environment that we used to know as school. They are now at home, where we can't control every component of their day to ensure success. They are now being asked to create their own agendas that balance the obligations of family and school. Students are now trying to troubleshoot technology difficulties on their own and they are looking for guidance. The comforts of brick-and-mortar school are gone and we are now learning how to navigate what schooling looks like in a remote environment. This is an opportunity for educators to change the way we teach and embrace a different way of learning.

11

Balancing and Staying Connected With Your PLN

Nyree Clark

I can do this! I am at one of the biggest technology conferences in the United States, the International Society for Technology in Education, also known by its abbreviated form of ISTE. San Antonio is home of ISTE 2017, with about 15,000 people in attendance. This is an annual gathering place for educators, leaders, and students to come together to acquire new ways to leverage technology for teaching and learning. I am the only person present from my department in my school district. I have *nobody* to eat lunch with, *nobody* to attend sessions with, *nobody* to explore the Exhibition Hall with, and *nobody* to share this experience with.

"I got this!," I think to myself. I am here to learn and I will focus on that. Take a deep breath, find your session, and relax. This is the time to curate as much information as you can to take back to your district and share with others.

And then it happened ... I checked Twitter. I was trying to look as casual and unaffected as possible as I was gathering my plan of attack for the day. My heart was racing from all the unknowns of the day. Where is my session? Will I make it there in time? I don't have anyone to save a spot for me. Will I be the only person that looks like me in every session? All of these questions were making me anxious until I remembered something I can control. I knew I could get information from Twitter. Maybe someone posted a good presenter to see. As my heart rate was starting to slow down to a normal pace I saw a tweet to win a free book from Matt Miller, @jmattmiller, for attending his session in the ViewSonic booth in the Exhibition Hall. A *free book!* Oh *yes! Let's do this.* I quickly made my way to the ViewSonic booth and found a seat before they were snatched up. As I sat down and collected myself from the mad sprint to the session to get a seat, I was overwhelmed by the amount of people around me talking about how they too found this information from the tweet that Matt Miller had posted on Twitter. "I wasn't the only person that saw that?" I thought. As I sat through the session I reflected on how many people were using Twitter to navigate the conference. Um, I hadn't thought about that. You mean you could actually use this platform for more than just finding resources?

But wait, it gets better! After the presentation Matt Miller had time to sign books for attendees. Oh my goodness! I would actually get to talk to him. I had been following him on Twitter for months and I admired the content he created and shared. I patiently waited my turn and while signing my book he actually talked to me. I couldn't believe *Matt Miller was talking to me!!!* Through this conversation we talked about our ISTE 2017 experiences, what our lives were like in our districts, and what we were looking forward to experiencing during the conference. We realized that we were both going to the same session and decided to walk there together. During this time, we shared our educational philosophies and our mutual connections. I quickly realized what I had been missing on Twitter was the interaction with the people I followed and my followers. I was not interacting with anyone. I was using Twitter like one would use Wikipedia or Google. Find, search, locate, and sometimes retweet is all I ever did. I didn't realize it then, but what we were actually doing was starting my personal learning network (PLN). That is how my PLN started, and it has been one of the single most impactful events of my teaching career.

What Is a PLN?

A PLN is a personal learning network; it is also called a personalized learning network by many. Pay close attention to the evolution from *personal* to *personalized*. Your personalized learning network is not a random collection of people you know, but a personalized group of people with the same shared interest, goals, and focuses. A PLN is rooted in the principles of connectionism. Learning is enhanced when an individual is able to form meaningful associations with others. Various social media platforms are used to provide people a place to communicate, collaborate, create, challenge, empower, and support each other through ongoing learning goals.

Purpose of a PLN

In 2016 my school district hired 18 teachers on special assignment (TOSAs). I interviewed and was hired to be a reading interventionist with a side of technology integration. My new job came with new responsibilities and workflow. Working with students came naturally to me, but supporting teachers from preschool to 6th grade was a new skill set to acquire. There was absolutely no one on my school campus that understood what I was going through. Where could I get support? Who could share best practices and be a thought partner as I worked through some situations I was going through? There were actually hundreds of people going through exactly what I was going through, and I found them on Twitter. I was able to join a live weekly discussion called a Twitter chat. The moderators of the chat I participated in, @TOSACHAT, were all TOSAs at the time, and there was not one but hundreds of people offering suggestions, resources, and direct messages for further collaboration with me through this weekly chat.

That is the purpose of a PLN. This is a community you will be able to access as a global think tank with your ideas and projects. It is open collaboration at its best. There are no time constraints. You can communicate with people asynchronously

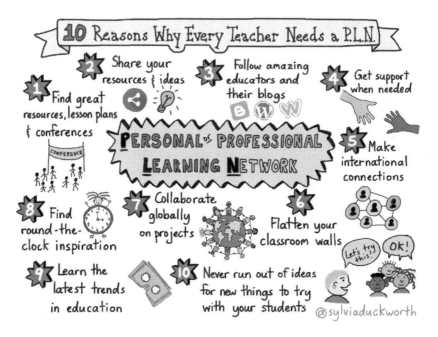

FIGURE 11.1 Ten reasons why every teacher needs a PLN.

Source: Image used with permission of Sylvia Duckworth

as well as synchronously. There is no better way to gain perspective on what you are doing than with engaging in a PLN. You will get immediate feedback on your contributions to the community and will continue to grow and build relationships with the people you follow as well as the people that follow you. PLNs accept people for the ideas they share and not for the titles they possess. This is truly a network of reflection and collaboration that drives the force of the PLN. Figure 11.1, a sketchnote created by Sylyvia Duckworth, showcases ten reasons why every teacher needs a personal/professional learning network.

PLN Challenges

A PLN is not a one-shot fix. You will not be able to create a PLN and leave it unattended and expect it to grow and flourish. PLNs are collaborative and will grow as much as they are watered, so to speak. Meaning, with effort your PLN will expand. Another challenge for educators new to building a PLN is the level of digital skills they possess. There are plenty of platforms for you to choose from. Start with the tool that is most comfortable for you to use or one that your district is promoting. My former superintendent, Jerry Almendarez, suggested we use Twitter as a means for us to "tell our stories." Since my district promoted Twitter, I created a Twitter account to build my PLN with my district in mind. Mr. Almendarez shared that we all have a story to tell and it is important to be the person to shape that narrative. Imagine taking a picture of two of your students working on a collaborative digital slideshow. You write a quick description of what they are doing and post the picture on your social media platforms. Included in that post is the content they are learning, the technology tool being used, and the skill they are actively engaged in. This is an example of sharing your story. You are not expecting your students to go home and correctly retell what happened at school. You have carefully crafted the narrative of what is taking place inside your classroom along with your thoughts, feelings, and teaching philosophies. Your caregivers will know exactly what type of learning environment their child resides in by the information or stories you provide.

Another challenge may be fear of putting yourself out there in the world. I know it can be a bit intimidating in the beginning, but remember that you are actively seeking people you know are supportive of you right where you are. A PLN is there for support, not to tear you down. You may also lack knowledge or are unfamiliar with topics you may encounter. Do not let that be your reason for not starting a PLN. It is just the opposite. Join a PLN to learn more about an unknown subject. There will be educators waiting and willing to connect with you.

Benefits of a PLN

Your PLN belongs to you. There is no district mandate on who you have to follow, what you need to learn, or what you have to do with that information once it's obtained. Your PLN is all yours. You control your own professional development. Think of it like your own 20% project, in which you have the good fortune of working on your project for 20% of the time. You get to explore your passions, interests, and unknown subjects, but you're not alone. You actually have other people to share the experience with.

Learning happens around-the-clock in your PLN. There is a flexibility you have to connect when it suits your needs. You can connect synchronously like in a Twitter chat that is happening at the same time for anyone joining that event. During this time, you are having a live discussion with the world. It is a phenomenal event to be a part of. The amount of collaboration is unparalleled to anything else that happens in that short amount of time with that many people speaking at once.

One of my favorite aspects of being a part of a PLN is the global connections you make. During the ISTE 2017 conference I was introduced to Flipgrid for the first time. I do not want to lie to you, I did feel like I was not being loyal to Seesaw when I visited the Flipgrid booth at the Exhibition Hall, but the things we will do for a raffle prize! The connection was automatic with Flipgrid. My focus for ISTE 2017 was looking at how I could improve student engagement in my small intervention groups. Talking with Flipgrid about building engagement and student voice was powerful for me. They shared many of the same educational philosophies as me and offered a plethora of resources, ideas, strategies, and other people for me to connect with to continue the collaboration.

Flipgrid is located in Minneapolis and the time difference does not deter from their willingness to work with people all over the globe. When Flipgrid created their #SOLIDGOLDenState Flipgrid Bus Tour, they made sure to include Crestmore Elementary School as a stop on their route to the Spring CUE Conference of 2019. The relationships created and fostered between Flipgrid and the teachers at Crestmore is what brought their Student Voice Bus Tour to a school in my district.

Twitter is where the relationship grows through comments, shared resources, Twitter chats, and project collaborations over the years. Yes, I said years. This relationship took time to develop and so will your PLN. It isn't something that happens overnight, but will develop and grow with you as your interest grows, changes, and evolves with your job, expectations, and worldviews.

How to Build a PLN

The first step in building a PLN is doing some research to learn more about it. Use the resources at bit.ly/PLNresources2020 as a starting place for you to begin your PLN journey. Figure 11.2 outlines four steps in growing a personal/professional learning network.

Follow these three easy steps to starting or growing your own PLN:

Step 1: Social Media

◆ Connect with people on Twitter. Search for people with your similar interests. If you are interested in EdTech you may want to follow @JakeMillerTech, @CitiCoach, @educopilot, and @deelanier.

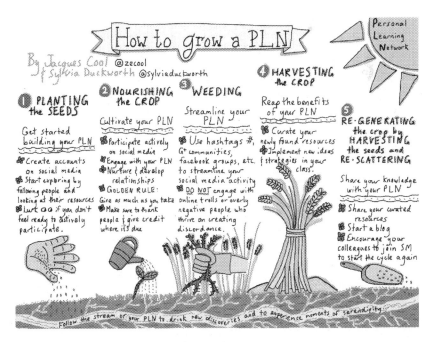

FIGURE 11.2 How to grow a PLN.

Source: Image used with permission of Sylvia Duckworth

♦ If you are looking for pedagogy and social justice you can connect with @k_shelton, @cultofpedagogy, @RaceEmbrace, and @Tolerance_org.

♦ If you are looking to connect and learn more about EdTech tools there is @Flipgrid, @wakelet, @Seesaw, and @Screencastify.

♦ Do you need templates? Connect with @TsGiveTs, @DitchThatTxtbk, and @KVoge71.

♦ Connect with people on Facebook. Facebook has groups that specialize in select areas. There are groups like the HyperDocs group that allow you to share resources, Seesaw for Educators if you're a Seesaw user, EdTech ambassador groups, and groups dedicated to content-specific publishers' content and resources like Wonders ELA or Go Math. Facebook has many dynamic teacher groups that foster a place for collaboration, sharing ideas, and resources. On Facebook you can search for groups by clicking the icon that shows a group of people or you can type the name of a group you are looking for in the search window.

♦ Instagram and LinkedIn are also valuable social media sites. They will allow you an opportunity to follow people for content, resources, and communication.

♦ Voxer is a walkie-talkie app that allows the user to leave voice messages, images, or text messages asynchronously. Voxer is great for people that like to talk and have an asynchronous conversation.

Each platform discussed here holds a different function for the user. Twitter is for quickly sharing information, Facebook has a conversational tone, and Voxer allows people to connect verbally.

Step 2: Chats and Educational Blogs

♦ Twitter chats are a meeting place for people to gather and discuss shared topics. They typically last anywhere from 30 minutes to one hour. Chats allow you to connect with hundreds of people at one time in a live discussion focused on the same topic. Don't forget to follow the people that will help you grow. #TosaChat, #Ditch-book, and #CueChat are fantastic chats for EdTech and coaching.

◆ Educational blogs (EduBlogs) are blog posts that are written to amplify best practices in education. There are countless blogs out there, so you need to search for the information that will help you excel. You will be able to learn, share, curate, and collaborate on different topics. I love to learn from Educazen.org and CultofPedagogy.com. There are always quick tips and resources. I also benefit from Innovating Play, which features a blog post, resources, as well as a slow Flipgrid chat for educators that work with grades PreK to 2nd grade.

Step 3: Conferences and Networks

◆ Attending a conference is another way to build your PLN. When you attend sessions, you are able to connect with your presenters. There are various gatherings where you can meet up with like-minded people and make connections. Some of my favorite conferences are ISTE and CUE. Don't forget to reach out to your local affiliate groups. It will be easy to grow your PLN there.

◆ Network, network, network. Joining a club, group, or team that encourages growth in your area of expertise will surely grow your PLN. You will have opportunities to connect with leaders in your field and this could lead to collaboration opportunities, brainstorming ideas, and creating resources to grow in your craft.

I encourage you to not work alone in your career. Set aside 10 to 20 minutes a day to collaborate and interact with your PLN. Build connections with people, share your work, and share resources. Build a community that will inspire, uplift, and empower you. While attending one conference I was able to make connections with some amazing people that have made a huge impact on my pedagogy and career. We have grown together in the last three years and have become professional friends. It doesn't stop there. As I grow in my interests, I add new members to my

PLN. I also edit interests that are no longer a focus or goal. As your job interests, grade level, or personal views change, you will find that you may need to connect with different people to drive a new level of collaboration and conversation that you had not experienced before. No one person has the answers to every question, but together our community of learners will excel as we lift each other up and learn from one another. That is how we model being #BetterTogether.

I Am Connected, Now What?

In 2013 the US Department of Education named October Connected Educator Month. During this month educators are encouraged to use their technology skills to participate in online events and build PLNs. The internet allows us limitless access to connections to other people and resources. Listed below are some key ideas to help you stay connected and thriving in your PLN.

- ◆ Twitter remains the driving force of a PLN. The information is constantly flowing and connections are reinforced through feedback and reflection.
- ◆ Build a core circle of educators you want to learn with and from. Stay connected with them by creating a list on Twitter that will allow you to follow the feeds that are most important to you.
- ◆ Join Facebook Live, Twitter chats, and webinars to connect with other like-minded people and meet new educators.
- ◆ Be an active participant and ask questions. Ask open-ended questions that will elicit a variety of responses from your community.
- ◆ Remember to cite your sources and acknowledge contributions made from others in your community. It is a sign of respect to have your work recognized and shared with others. When you share your voice with others it will allow people to connect with you on a deeper level.
- ◆ Create professional and personal accounts to make it easier for you to facilitate your social media. My Twitter

account is where my professional life lives and my Instagram and Facebook are personal private accounts. When you designate your accounts, you will find that splitting your screen time will be easier to monitor.

The hashtag may be what originally brought you to Twitter and the people you connect with will keep you there. When I first created my Twitter account, I only followed people and retweeted their resources. It took me over a year to feel comfortable to add to the conversation. Why the shift? My PLN was asking for more of me and I was comfortable in the safe space I had created online with them. While at ISTE 2017 I met many fantastic professionals that have now become some of my best friends and collaborative partners. We make time to connect on a personal level as well as professionally. The relationships you build are a give and take of ideas, dreams, and goals. Building each other up to be the best educators you can possibly be is the epitome of being better together. A productive PLN *will not* let you fail. They will offer support and advice to help you reach your objectives.

Remember that building a PLN is not a sprint but a marathon. Take your time to build connections with others and grow in the areas that make your heart smile. Your level of connectivity will ebb and flow with your work and life responsibilities. If you need some time for self-care to recharge your energy, take it. Your PLN is not a competition for the most likes, followers, or retweets. Your PLN is a group of people and followers that want to see you thrive, achieve, and accomplish your goals as you support them to thrive, achieve, and accomplish their goals. I leave you to reflect on this quote and know it is never too late to create a PLN.

One does not need to be connected to be a good educator, but if one is a good educator, being connected can make him, or her a better, and a more relevant educator.
—Tom Whitby, EduBlogs

Printed in the United States
By Bookmasters